TEST YOUR

COACHING SKILLS

I.Q.

Prepared by Dennis C. Kinlaw, Ed.D.

Coaching for Commitment: Managerial Strategies for Obtaining Superior Performance

Dennis C. Kinlaw, Ed.D.

University Associates, Inc.

8517 Production Avenue
San Diego, California 92121

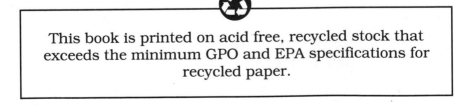

For Christiana, my first and best coach.

Table of Contents

Introduction

B uilding employee commitment is the key to obtaining sustained, superior performance. This book is about coaching—one strategy that every manager can employ to build employee commitment. The book is based on my fifteen years of experience in teaching the value and skills of coaching to hundreds of managers and supervisors. It presents coaching as a management strategy that has special usefulness for organizations facing today's intense competition in the marketplace for their products and services.

The Manager's Job: Limits of the Control Model

Managers and supervisors are responsible for producing results—achieving production quotas, developing new products, meeting sales goals, ensuring technical excellence, solving problems in complex systems, and completing an almost endless variety of projects. Although managers often contribute directly to results through their technical competence, they produce most results *indirectly* through the wills and competencies of others.

"Achieving results through other people" has become a standard description of the work of managers and supervisors. This definition is, however, inadequate and misleading because it assumes that managers can directly control the performance of others to obtain desired outcomes. The key is the word "desired." If managers and organizations can establish enough policies, enforce enough rules, and invoke effective rewards and punishments, and if they practice rigorous oversight and appraisal of performance, they may achieve a *satisfactory* level of performance. But no one really believes that satisfactory, or average, performance is good enough. In a world of international competition, if managers accept satisfactory performance, they inevitably accept a loss in competitiveness, a decline in market share, stagnant capital growth, and decreasing profitability.

People may conform, i.e., do satisfactory work, because they are forced to. They only do *superior* work because they *want to.*

During a recent series of productivity seminars, I asked each group of managers and employees to respond to two questions: "How many of you think your boss would notice if you put fifteen percent *more* effort into your jobs?" and "How many of you think your boss would notice if you put fifteen percent *less* effort into your jobs?" The 1,500 respondents were almost unanimous in replying that their bosses would not notice if their work varied by fifteen percent effort either way.

It is apparent that all of us have control of an enormous amount of discretionary time and energy. We can give a good bit more to our jobs or we can give a good bit less and, in general, we are the only ones who know. This discretionary time and energy is what makes the difference between satisfactory and superior performance.

Strategies for Improving Performance Through Commitment

The *desired* level of performance is not merely "satisfactory." The desired level is *superior* and *outstanding*. But superior and outstanding performance is generated by the performers, because they control the discretionary time and energy that make the difference. The question, then, is how managers can tap this discretionary reservoir of potential in order to obtain superior performance.

We are witnessing a major shift in management philosophy and practice. The shift is away from managing by control toward managing by commitment. All the major strategies that have improved performance in this country over the past ten years have this in common: they all have increased employee *commitment* to quality and productivity.

There are a number of such strategies. One is to increase the involvement of employees in developing new ideas, in doing work-group planning, and in solving problems. Another is letting employees share in company profits. A third is to make employees directly responsible for whole units of output, such as is the case in leaderless groups and production teams. Coaching is another effective strategy, and it can be used independently or in conjunction with the others. What all these strategies have in common is that they succeed in developing employee commitment to results based on a personal sense of ownership, i.e., the feeling that the product or service is theirs.

Outline of this Book

This book contains five chapters. A brief overview of each chapter follows.

- *Chapter One. Building Commitment.* Chapter I explores the meaning of commitment; discusses the visible evidences of commitment; and shows how coaching occupies a central and dominant role in building employee commitment.

- *Chapter Two. A Definition of Coaching.* This chapter answers the question "What is coaching?" It explains the four different functions of coaching, identifies the criteria for successful coaching, and provides a definition of successful coaching. It also gives the two major reasons why managers fail in coaching.

- *Chapter Three. Coaching Process 1: Solving Problems.* A major premise of this book is that coaching must be understood and used as a *process*. Chapter Three describes the general characteristics of the coaching process. It tells how the three coaching functions of counseling, mentoring, and tutoring are managed through Coaching Process 1, and how the fourth coaching function of confronting is managed through Coaching Process 2. The rest of the chapter is devoted to a detailed description of Process 1, solving problems.

- *Chapter Four. Coaching Process 2: Improving Performance.* Confronting is the coaching function managed by Process 2. In this chapter, important distinctions are made between confronting and criticizing. It also tells how managers make confronting unnecessarily difficult. Then Process 2 is described, along with its similarities to and differences from Process 1.

- *Chapter Five. Coaching and Superior Leadership.* This chapter is the summary and conclusion to the book. It presents some of my conclusions about superior leadership and explains how critical the role of coaching is for superior management performance.

Targeted Readers

This book is written, first of all, for managers. It reflects my fifteen years of experience observing managers coach, investigating the practice of coaching, and teaching managers the processes and skills for successful coaching.

"Manager," in this book, refers to those persons in organizations who have formal responsibility for the performance of others or who must depend on others in order to do their own jobs. This includes supervisors, leads, and key staff people, as well as those with the title of manager.

Most of what is said about coaching in this book also will apply to anyone who has responsibility for the performance of some other person, e.g., teachers who manage the learning of students and parents who manage the behavior of their children.

This book also is intended as a resource for HRD professionals who have responsibility for developing, delivering, or marketing programs on coaching. The book gives instructors the conceptual basis needed to conduct coaching workshops. A note to trainers about forthcoming materials to be used in conducting such workshops is found at the end of this book.

Employee commitment is the key to superior performance, and coaching is a potent strategy for building such commitment. Teaching managers the processes of coaching presents human resource development (HRD) professionals with a special opportunity to shape the practices of managers to meet today's performance demands.

Chapter One.
Building Commitment

T he central theme of this book is that employee commitment
is the key to superior performance and that coaching can be
a powerful strategy for building commitment.

The Meaning of Commitment

Commitment, like motivation, is not something that we can observe
directly. We infer that they exist because of what people say and
do. There are at least two kinds of behavior that signal employee
commitment. First, committed employees appear to be very single-
minded or focused in doing their work. The second characteristic
that we associate with committed employees is their willingness
to make personal sacrifices to reach their team's or organization's
goals.

Focus

Drake, an aeronautics engineer, is described by his colleagues as
"the most committed researcher around." They delight in telling
stories to illustrate what they mean.

> • Drake has been known to get up in the middle of a meal or a party,
> without excusing himself, and go back to his wind tunnel to work on
> a problem or some new idea that suddenly occurred to him.
> • Sometimes Drake becomes so preoccupied with his work that he
> forgets for months to deposit his paychecks. One time he went so long

that the people from disbursing tracked him down, found his paychecks stuffed in various drawers of his desk, and took them to his bank and deposited them just to straighten out their own records.

• You can never tell when Drake will show up at the facility, and you can never tell when he might leave. No one ever makes a luncheon appointment with him and really expects him to keep it. He could be walking with you and be halfway to the cafeteria, and then he will just turn around and start back to his office.

One of the things we mean by "committed" people is that they have a focus. Sometimes this focus is so intense that it seems as though they have on blinders or suffer from tunnel vision. From the time that the Challenger accident occurred, everyone at NASA's Kennedy Space Center was focused on launching the next shuttle. The director's recurring theme was, "Our ten top priorities are return to flight, return to flight, return to flight. . . ."

Children at play give a very clear example of what focus and commitment mean. Every parent knows how difficult it is to interrupt children when they are involved in a game or building with blocks or painting. Parents often must resort to threats to get their children to stop for meals.

Some years ago, I was consulting to a part of the old "Ma Bell" system and I was impressed by the single focus that all the employees had in regard to their jobs. Whenever I asked employees what they were responsible for, their answers were typically the same. Whether a person was in purchasing or installation or was a member of a line crew, the answer was: "My job is dial tone." These employees were committed to the overarching goal of the company. They believed that getting dial tone for the customer and restoring dial tone took precedence over everything else. Dial tone was the symbol for a working phone system and it was always their number-one priority.

I recently interviewed a group of project managers. These people typically work in a matrix organization. The people they utilize to achieve objectives may be working on several projects at the same time and belong ultimately to functional managers. Project managers must compete with other project managers and the rest of the organization for people and resources. One of the questions that I asked these managers was, "What do you think is the most important quality or attribute that a project manager must have in order to be successful?" In one way or another all of them said that project managers must believe that what they are doing is the most important thing in the company and that if they lose their commitment to their own goals or question their importance, they are lost.

Any manager who has tried to ensure "zero defects" in an organization's services or products knows that nothing happens until the people who do the work care about its quality. Creating quality-improvement programs can educate people about quality and, for the short term, create a focus on quality. Quality-assurance inspections can provide a way to track defects and identify systemic problems. Quality-circle programs can develop small-group competencies for identifying and solving performance problems. But nothing short of each individual's devotion to quality in every one of his or her tasks makes the difference over the long haul.

Over an extended period of time, managers can teach their workers to disregard quality. Managers can be so concerned about quotas and so fearful of missing schedules that they can teach their workers the same fear and concern with only numbers and profit. By insisting that purchasing take the low bid and buy at the lowest price, managers have forced production workers and researchers alike to work with inferior materials and to produce work that they knew was inferior and which they detested.

However, people are naturally predisposed to be committed to quality. *Systems do not produce quality; people do.* They can produce it despite poor systems. They can produce it without supervision, and they can produce it despite poor management and supervision. The role of managers is to free people so that they can exercise their commitment to quality without fear.

While having some tires replaced on my car recently, I had an enviable experience. First, the store manager explained in detail the three brands of tires that came in the size I needed. He talked about road noise and life expectancy under various driving conditions. After he determined my typical driving pattern, he recommended the least expensive of the three brands. After the tires were put on and balanced, the manager insisted that I take the car for a short drive to see if I detected any problems. Finally, he gave me a detailed description of the warranty and follow-up service. I was told that if I had a flat tire within fifty miles of the store, I could just call for free road service. Ten days after I purchased the tires, the mechanic who installed them called me to see if I was completely satisfied.

The focus that is characteristic of commitment usually results in quality.

Personal Sacrifice

Probably the one sure measure of the strength of a commitment is how willing a person is to make personal sacrifices to meet the commitment. There is a limit, of course, in the degree of sacrifice that a person can make. However, it is impossible to predict what this limit will be.

When the manager of NASA's Viking Project announced that there was to be "no leave until launch," no one quibbled. Even when he said in the December prior to launch that "Christmas is a working day," no one really expected it to be otherwise.

The corollary to sacrifice is *meaning*. People will not invest themselves in a task if it does not connect to their values and if it does not provide them with a sense of achievement. People sacrifice most for whatever contributes to their sense of personal worth.

One slogan that illustrates the relationship between commitment and sacrifice was related by a man who played football for Vince Lombardi. He said that one of Lombardi's favorite dictums was: "If you can't play hurt, you can't play."

The complaints that I hear managers make most often about the service and administrative functions in their organizations are that the people in these functions are not committed to the bottom line and that they do not have the big picture. These managers may be right, but they do not see their own responsibility for the problem. Two examples can help to illustrate this point.

> During a consulting job with an East Coast insulation firm, I was asked to resolve some of the conflicts that had arisen between the home office and the field teams. I discovered that none of the people in finance, accounting, or purchasing had ever seen their mechanics at work. They had never seen what the company "did." How could they possibly feel commitment to the service that the company provided if they had no connection to it? How could they understand the frustration of the mechanics if they had never seen them working in hot, dirty, cramped, overhead spaces insulating heat ducts? It took only a

few visits to the field by the people from the home office to turn the situation around. When both the office people and the field people were committed to the same concept of the firm's service, the conflict disappeared.

A common practice in engineering firms is to have the lowest echelons submit "weekly notes"; these notes go to the next level and then to the next level until they reach the top. At each level the notes are reviewed, edited, reduced, or expanded. It is not uncommon for the people at the bottom (who started the process) never to see the finished product, never to receive credit for their contributions, never to receive feedback of any kind. In these same organizations, a frequent remark from managers is, "I can never seem to get people to submit their notes on time." These managers are complaining about a lack of commitment, but how can they hope to gain commitment from people who are asked to perform a task that is like dropping stones into a bottomless pit?

The message from these examples is that if we want people to share the same commitment to the company's objectives and operations, then we must make them aware of what those objectives and operations are. Commitment follows meaning. A job is only a job until one identifies with it and sees the meaning in what one is doing; then it becomes a commitment. People do not sacrifice unless what they are doing has meaning. People need to connect what they do to some larger whole. In work, people need to know how they contribute to their organization's success.

In summary, commitment is evident in the focus that people exhibit toward a goal, and the surest measure of commitment is in the personal sacrifices that people are willing to make to achieve the goal.

Building Commitment

If one of a manager's primary tasks is to create commitment and focus in employees, then the manager must have a clear idea of just what commitment is and what contributes to it. It may be useful to visualize commitment as a solid block that rests on four sturdy supports, or legs (see Figure 1). The four supports of commitment are as follows:

- Clarity about goals and values;
- Employee competencies that allow success;
- The degree of influence that employees have; and
- The expressed appreciation given to employees for their contributions.

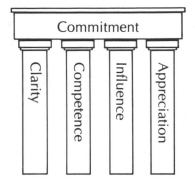

Figure 1. The Supports of Commitment

Clarity

Formal and explicit strategic planning has become a common activity in most organizations. Informal and implicit strategic planning has always been around. McDonnell Douglas has done formal strategic planning only recently. But so long as "Mr. Mac" was at the helm, he knew where the company was going, and his employees knew that he knew.

Strategic planning (when it is effective) does at least two things: it clarifies what the organization intends to be and it clarifies what the organization intends to be like. The first part of this statement has to do with the organization's vision, goals, and strategies. The second part has to do with the organization's core values.

Effective planning can be done at every level of the organization. I know of organizations in which strategic planning is given only lip service at the top, so first-level supervisors do their own. I know of pockets in organizations in which values such as cooperation and loyalty to one another are intense, despite their general absence in the larger organization.

For commitment to a job to exist, an employee must have a focus. Focus is created by communicating the strategic goals and core values of the organization downward through each level. At each level, these goals and values must be translated into the work and decisions of each manager and employee.

> A friend of mine who heads an electronics research group personally holds a two- or three-hour coaching session with each new employee. He presents in great detail the history of the organization. He describes its evolving nature and he talks about its culture. He spends most of his time ensuring that the new employee understands what his organization believes about people, about freedom in research, about mutual respect, and about accountability—the core values of the organization.

> My dentist has a set of professional beliefs displayed in the waiting room. I look forward to going to the dentist with about as much joy as anyone does. So it is a real comfort to me in that waiting room to read, "We believe in painless dentistry." The good news is that both the dentists and the technicians really do believe it. Before, during, and after each procedure, they are solicitous of my well being. I am sure that these dentists see fewer patients during the day than their competitors, but judging by how long it takes to get an appointment, these people are not hurting for revenue.

It is impossible to overestimate the importance of establishing and communicating organizational values. It is equally impossible to measure the confusion and loss in performance that is created when values are *not* communicated or, worse, are communicated and then not adhered to.

Values bring clarity *if they are real*. Managers cannot talk about quality and then, every time there is a crunch, reinforce the fact that schedules and quotas are the true drivers. Managers cannot tell foremen that quality is number one and then burn them every time they stop production.

Of course, few managers work in the ideal organization. Some of us work in companies that do little or nothing at the top to communicate strategic goals and core values. The lack of such communication does not, however, change the equation. Without clarity there can be no focus, and without a focus there will not be commitment.

One of the key activities that I have supervisors and their subordinates undertake in a team-development workshop is to answer the following:

- What is your number-one purpose as a work group?
- What makes this purpose important?
- What are the actual values that currently drive your work group's performance?
- What are the values that you would like to drive your work group's performance?

The results of these workshops have demonstrated that greater clarity can be brought to any level of an organization. It is a lot easier, of course, when there is clarity at the top. But all the sins of top management need not be visited on all the lower levels of the organization. Every manager can do something.

Commitment is evidenced in the purposeful, focused behavior of employees who are willing to make sacrifices in order to ensure quality work or success. This focus can be created only if managers build clarity about their work group's purpose and its values. However, announcing goals and values in a work group or organization does not mean that they take hold and actually influence what people do. The only way that goals and values become clear, functional influences is for them to be personally communicated and reinforced by managers. Coaching, as a one-to-one interaction between managers and employees, is a primary strategy for building clarity.

Competence

People develop commitment toward what they believe they can do well. People do not like to fail. They will try to avoid the things that they think they cannot do. If managers want commitment, they must make sure that employees have the ability and willingness to be successful in their jobs. There are two elements that managers must address in building employee competence.

- They must ensure that their employees have the knowledge, skills, and experience to perform their tasks, and

- They must ensure that their employees have the confidence to perform their tasks.

My work with organizations has convinced me that managers do not always place improving the competencies of their subordinates high on their list of priorities or responsibilities. I have asked thousands of managers, "What do you produce—what are you responsible for?" Far and away the most frequent answers are "surveys, software, reports, quotas, safety, service, profit, new business, completed work packages, cost savings," etc. Rarely do the answers suggest that developing employees is high on a manager's list of responsibilities.

Some managers even object to the idea that they are responsible for developing employees. They say such things as: "It's their responsibility to develop themselves"; "Nobody made it easy for me, so why should it be easy for them?"; and "On company time, they do their jobs, and if they want to learn something, they can do it on their own time."

No one can quarrel seriously with the idea that individuals have final responsibility to develop themselves. But not to see the development of people as a fundamental management responsibility is shortsighted and foolish. It is not unlike saying that all resources in an organization should renew themselves or that technology should improve itself.

The point is not simply that developing people is the way that human competence is assured for doing the business of today and tomorrow. Developing competence also is fundamental to building commitment. Each of us feels a great deal more commited, i.e., willing to do our best, when we are tasked with jobs that we know we can do well or that we know we can learn to do well. Managers who help employees to increase their knowledge, skill, and experience also are building employee commitment—the key to sustained, superior performance.

What are the ways to build competence? Obviously, there is training—classroom training, on-the-job training, cross-training, etc. Some organizations have extensive training programs or tuition-reimbursement programs. Some support professional programs in which employees take several months or more away from their regular jobs and do a tour of duty at some other part of the firm. Many organizations now have computer centers and learning centers.

The most personal strategy for building competence—and, therefore, one of the most powerful—is coaching. It is the one sure way in which managers can find out exactly what their employees do not know and what they need to know. Coaching also is a way to provide support and reassurance to employees who are taking on new tasks. Coaching facilitates learning because it is timely and focuses on exactly what the individual employee needs to know.

Influence

Influence is the third "leg" of commitment. Employees do not perform nearly as well when they are consistently denied any input in their jobs and are expected to follow unquestionably the decisions of their leaders. Managers who deny employees any influence get the results they deserve. These results range from boredom to passive resistance or even sabotage. Many employees end up doing what they are told to do, but they do it exactly and they do no more. One of my favorite cartoons shows a supervisor who is wild-eyed and pulling his hair. Underneath the cartoon is the caption: "Oh my God, he did what I told him to!" Influence breeds ownership, and ownership breeds commitment.

Extending influence to employees can happen in a number of ways. It can happen through "talk back to the boss" programs or it can take the shape of formal employee-suggestion programs. It can happen by means of small groups and special teams such as quality circles, production teams, and advisory groups. It may be extended through the informal and ongoing conversations that managers have with subordinates.

To illustrate how important influence is in developing employee commitment to improvement and sustained, superior performance, think about organizations in which members have the most influence, such as research organizations and "think tanks." Then think about organizations in which members have the least influence, such as prisons. How much commitment do prisoners have to the superior performance of their guards and to achieving the goal of the organization—their successful incarceration?

One way in which I have helped managers begin to extend influence to their subordinates is based on the model presented in

Figure 2. The model suggests that there are three areas for influence and three kinds of influence within each area.

1. Innovation	2. Planning	3. Problem Solving
• Inputting	• Inputting	• Inputting
• Deciding	• Deciding	• Deciding
• Implementing	• Implementing	• Implementing

Figure 2. Opportunities To Extend Employee Influence

Innovation

Innovation is the process of developing and implementing new ideas. Managers involve subordinates and co-workers in the process of innovation through the following:

- Inputting—encouraging them to present new ideas;
- Decision making—permitting them to help decide which ideas will be tested or developed;
- Implementing—helping them to test and gain support for new ideas.

It takes discipline to encourage new ideas. A friend of mine has collected what he calls "show-stopping ways to kill innovation." He has recorded the kinds of comments that some managers make in response to new ideas. Here are eight of my favorites.

- "Our problem is different."
- "There are pros and cons."
- "Let's be realistic."
- "Let's study it."

- "It conflicts with policy."
- "The boss won't like it."
- "We tried that once before."
- "This is not the right time to try it."

Planning

Managers also can extend the opportunities of subordinates and co-workers to participate in the various planning processes of the organization, e.g., work planning, budget planning, planning organizational changes, developing work-group goals, etc. Subordinates and co-workers can be involved in three ways:

- •Inputting—having them provide information, data, and suggestions for budgets, team goals, planned changes, etc.;
- •Decision making—using team decision making in developing plans;
- •Implementing—having them select strategies for implementing plans, evaluating plans, and modifying plans.

Problem Solving

A final way in which managers can extend influence to subordinates and co-workers is by giving them the chance to work on problems in three different ways:

- Inputting—identifying problems, researching data, providing technical information and expertise;
- Decision making—participating in decisions about problem definition, about which problems will be addressed, etc.:
- Implementing—designing solutions, undertaking and evaluating strategies, etc.

Coaching is the key for extending the influence of employees. In their coaching conversations with employees, managers permit employees actively to identify their own needs and to help shape the ways these needs are met. Coaching can involve employees in setting their own performance expectations and their own career goals. It can actively engage them in finding ways to improve their jobs and their performance. It can, in short, become the primary management strategy for extending to employees the chance to influence what happens to them and their jobs.

Appreciation

The fourth leg that supports commitment is appreciation. One of my untested theories is that if you want to know how people feel about their organization and their work, check the bathrooms.

> In one place in which I periodically do consulting, the bathrooms always are immaculate. One time the "being cleaned" sign was out, so I took the opportunity to compliment the janitor. Then I asked him, "Why do you always do such a great job?" He answered, "Because I know everyone appreciates it being nice." I later found out that the senior manager in the building routinely takes time to thank the janitor for his work. Once he even prepared a letter of appreciation and took the janitor upstairs to receive it from the vice president!

Over the past three years, I have surveyed a dozen organizations to determine employees' perceptions of five variables that we know predict an organizations' performance. These variables are clarity, fairness, responsiveness, involvement, and appreciation. The variable that employees are most likely to be least positive about (to perceive as occurring the least) is appreciation.

A "tough-minded" manager said to me once: "Where I come from, the appreciation that you get for doing a good job is that you get to keep your job." In today's world, this simply does not work. Commitment to superior performance is a function of clarity, competence, influence, *and* appreciation. People work best when they believe that what they do matters to someone else—especially their bosses.

The question is how to leverage acts of appreciation (especially the informal ones) so that they have the maximum impact. Of course, we need to recognize superior performance. But we need to recognize more than performance. Achievement is more than doing a job well. It may mean "hanging in there" when the going gets tough—such as surviving a reorganization or an IRS audit. It may mean being a loyal employee for ten or twenty years. It may mean doing some unrewarding, routine job over and over and still doing it well. It may even mean having the nerve to talk back to the boss. Employees often feel more appreciated for having their pain recognized than for having their performance recognized.

Another way to leverage appreciation is to make it personal. A young engineer whom I know has a framed envelope hanging on her wall. Across the top of the envelope is scrawled, "DATA-ANALYSIS BRANCH'S TOUGHING-IT-OUT AWARD." Underneath this is written, "Presented first to Jan Perkins for extraordinary courage and perseverance in the face of unwarranted and devastating criticism from the enemy." Jan received her award while making a presentation to a senior vice president who kept interrupting her with caustic comments and negative remarks. Jan's own supervisor tried to serve as a buffer and support her. When Jan sat down, her supervisor reached over her shoulder and presented her with the first DATA-ANALYSIS BRANCH TOUGHING-IT-OUT AWARD. One of the reasons why Jan valued this award so much was that it was one of a kind. It was distinctly and uniquely hers—a special response to her pain and hard work.

A third way to add clout to appreciation is to do something creative or even outrageous. "Hero of the Month" packs a lot more punch than "Employee of the Month." There could be a "Rookie of the Year" award for the best new employee. One executive hands out a "Zeal Seal" with a picture of the aquatic mammal as a background for his handwritten expression of thanks.

A fourth key to leveraging appreciation is to make it public. Some managers whom I know try to visit all their work areas at the end of each week to wrap things up, say "thank you," and provide encouragement. One manager does it in style. He tells his employees to stop working, then he asks one employee to stand with him as he gives a three- to five-minute commendation—or "doxology" as he calls it—to celebrate that person's contribution for the week.

The four things that support commitment are clarity, competence, influence, and appreciation. When managers ensure that all four are present in the work place, they develop employees who have the focus and the willingness to sacrifice that we call commitment.

The Special Role of Coaching

Throughout this chapter, I have suggested just how important coaching is for building commitment. Chapter 2 will present a formal definition of coaching, and subsequent chapters will explain in detail why coaching has a central and dominant role in building employee commitment and how it works.

In some organizations, everyone runs for cover when they see the boss coming. They know that their shortcomings will be exposed in painful detail or that they will get something else to do. In other organizations, they know that the visits from senior management are just window dressing. The executive asks a few general questions, barely pauses for a reply, and then moves on.

Most of us respond to the personal touch. We want our managers to know who we are and the special needs that we have. We want to be listened to when we make suggestions. We do not want to be taken for granted or simply told to fall in line when policies and organizational practices change.

Coaching is the process by which managers stay in touch with their subordinates. All the walking around in the world will not help managers to get the best from their employees unless they are walking around as coaches. *Coaching is eyeball-to-eyeball management.* Every conversation between managers and employees is potentially a coaching conversation. It is a chance to clarify goals, priorities, and standards of performance. It is a chance to reaffirm and reinforce the group's core values. It is a chance to hear ideas and to involve employees in the processes of planning and problem solving. More important than all the rest, it is a chance to say "thank you."

Key Learning Points for Chapter One

1. Employee commitment is the key to superior organizational performance. Commitment is evidenced by:

- Single-minded, focused behavior; and
- Willingness to sacrifice for the cause.

2. Commitment is supported by:

- Clarity about goals and values;
- Employee competencies that allow success;
- The degree of influence that employees have; and
- The expressed appreciation given to employees for their contributions.

3. Coaching is the key to employee commitment because it is face-to-face leadership that enables and facilitates. It frees up people so that they can do what they want to do: demonstrate their commitment to the best.

Chapter Two.
A Definition of Coaching

I did not realize just how varied the use of the term "coaching" was until I began to respond to clients' requests to teach their managers and supervisors how to coach. Some of these clients had in mind giving employees timely information about their performance or reviewing and adjusting performance expectations. Still others seemed to equate coaching with giving encouragement and inspiration—a kind of pep talk. The most common way, however, in which my clients talked about coaching was in terms of counseling, e.g., "performance counseling" or "performance coaching." Some requested a workshop on "coaching and counseling" and expected one topic to be covered, not two.

"Coaching" sometimes is used to describe a specific action such as encouraging, reinforcing, giving feedback, demonstrating, etc. At other times, it is used to denote the style of managers who have a developmental orientation toward employees and who manage by giving employees greater challenges, autonomy, and power.

This book focuses on coaching as a conversation. It is through four different types of conversations that coaching becomes apparent as a manager's dominant style.

The Four Coaching Functions

Confusion about coaching has probably come about precisely because it has been associated with other managerial conversations or functions such as, for example, counseling. Sometimes the term is used to describe something like mentoring—giving sage advice to a colleague or friend. At other times it is used to describe the process of tutoring—a one-on-one method of instruction. Over time, all three of these functions have, to varying degrees, become associated with coaching as a management practice.

In addition to the three similar functions of counseling, mentoring, and tutoring, managerial coaching includes the function of confronting employees to improve their performance. It is this function of confronting performance problems that gives coaching its most distinctive quality as part of a manager's job.

I believe that coaching is whatever the people who do it and whatever the people who train others to do it say that it is. However, the four functions of counseling, mentoring, tutoring, and confronting include most of the different activities that managers and training professionals have in mind when they use the term "coaching."

Generic Coaching

The fact that there are four different coaching functions suggests that coaching can have a number of different outcomes. For example, typical outcomes of *counseling* are:

- Accurate descriptions of problems and their causes;
- Technical and organizational insight;
- Venting of strong feelings;
- Changes in points of view;
- Commitment to self-sufficiency; and
- Deeper personal insight about one's feelings and behavior.

Typical outcomes of *mentoring* are:

- Development of political savvy;
- Sensitivity to the organization's culture;
- Personal networking;
- Greater proactivity in managing one's career;

- Commitment to the organization's goals and values; and
- Sensitivity to senior managers' likes and dislikes.

Typical outcomes from *tutoring* are:

- Increased technical competence;
- Increased breadth of technical understanding;
- Movement to expert status;
- Increased learning pace; and
- Commitment to continual learning.

Typical outcomes from *confronting* are:

- Clarification of performance expectations;
- Identification of performance shortfalls;
- Acceptance of more difficult tasks;
- Strategies to improve performance; and
- Commitment to continual improvement.

When we identify the four functions of coaching and then list numerous outcomes for each function, we seem to be suggesting that coaching is a very complex performance-management skill. In truth, the best thing about learning how to coach is that the same processes and skills are used in performing each function.

All four functions have so much in common that it is unnecessary and pointless for managers to learn how to counsel, how to mentor, how to tutor, and how to confront. Coaching should be learned and used as a generic management practice. As such, it can be adapted to all four functions and to every possible work environment.

Attributes of All Coaching Functions

All forms of coaching have two common attributes. These attributes are:

1. They are one-to-one conversations that
2. focus on performance or performance-related topics.

One-to-One

Coaching is a one-to-one conversation between a manager and an employee. This indicates that coaching is a personal conversation. It is based on the specific needs of the employee. If the conversation is not personal, it is not coaching.

In order to coach, the manager must discover the employee's personal needs. At times, every employee requires some sort of special, personal help. Coaching is a response to this personal need. It is an iterative process in which the manager discovers the employee's needs and then matches information, counsel, understanding, and resources to these needs. If it does not target these needs, the manager has missed the opportunity. The common mistake of many managers is that they spend so much time telling employees what they should know, what they should do, and how they should change that they waste the potential of the one-to-one characteristic of coaching.

Focus on Performance

Coaching conversations focus on performance. Performance, however, should not be understood as applying only to knowledge, skills, tasks, and objectives. It is the whole person who performs. Coaching includes any topic that concerns the employee as a person who performs. The underlying assumption of coaching is that managers can provide help to the employee. This help may be personal insight (counseling), political savvy (mentoring), learning (tutoring), or performance improvement (confronting). In all cases, the manager should help the employee to reach new levels of personal commitment for sustained, superior performance.

It is important to understand that there are no topics or problems that a manager should not discuss with an employee *if they affect the employee's work.* Of course, managers cannot help their employees to resolve all their problems. They cannot, for example, solve the

in not getting that report in on time" encourages the employee to feel guilty and apologetic. "I want to know when I can expect that report" requires the employee to take responsibility and to plan a change. "You're still making the same mistakes that we discussed last time" focuses the employee on failure. "Let's see what you've done since our last conversation and then go on to where you think you still need help" focuses the employee on success.

5. *Discipline.* One characteristic of the coaching processes that will be presented in this book is that they move through a series of interdependent stages. Undisciplined conversations do not follow specific stages. A common example is the ease with which managers start solving problems before they have developed sufficient information to even understand the problem. Another is how they give information about some action or procedure (tutoring) that is not helpful because the information is irrelevant to the employee's needs.

Criteria 4

Successful coaching follows an identifiable sequence or flow and requires the use of specific communication skills. Managers stipulate, monitor, review, revise, and assess results through a variety of formal and informal problem-solving transactions. It is these transactions that the manager influences most directly and which are most amenable to control, not the performance of the employee.

If by controlling we mean controlling the topics and content of a coaching conversation, then control is all but impossible because these conversations are with other people who also have some need to control. However, if we think of controlling as creating a *process* or flow that is satisfying to employees—one in which they willingly participate—then managers can exert significant control in coaching.

The term "process" describes a conversation that has the following characteristics:

- One or more specific purposes (such as those identified for the four coaching functions);

- Movement through certain predictable steps or stages that have their own goals;

- The use of special communication skills; and
- A result that is satisfying for all those involved.

Desired outcomes occur most consistently in coaching when managers concentrate on developing a satisfying process, rather than when they concentrate on controlling the content of the coaching conversation. Being an effective coach depends, then, on one's ability *to create and manage the process of a coaching conversation.* This is a central concept of this book.

The Two Processes of Coaching

Coaching in all of its functions takes two generic forms, both of which are processes. I call the first Process 1: Solving Problems and the second Process 2: Improving Performance. These two titles are somewhat arbitrary, but they provide a practical way of distinguishing and remembering the two processes.

Process 1: Solving Problems

Counseling, mentoring, and tutoring are coaching conversations that should follow the problem-solving process. This process starts with some employee need. It may be initiated by an employee, who requests some type of help from the manager, or it may be initiated by the manager, who offers some help to the employee.

The needs that employees have may bear directly or indirectly on performance. These needs may be ones that must be responded to immediately, e.g., help with a current project, clarification about conflicting priorities, or help with a personal crisis. Other needs may concern distant career goals, future professional experiences, or long-term learning projects.

Process 2: Improving Performance

Confronting is different from counseling, mentoring, and tutoring. Coaching conversations for improving performance are always initiated by a manager with the purpose of adjusting an employee's performance. The purpose may be to correct a deficiency or it may be to present the employee with a new task or job challenge for which the manager perceives that the employee is ready.

Successful Coaching: A Working Definition

All successful coaching conversations are directed toward improving performance and ensuring a commitment to sustained, superior performance. These results can be achieved only through the mutual development of information. Another outcome of successful coaching is the maintenance or improvement of a positive relationship between the manager and employee. Beside bearing directly on good performance, information is the basis for all positive relationships. Trust, candor, and cooperation all depend on both manager and subordinate sharing a common body of information.

The two coaching processes of solving problems and improving performance provide simple frameworks for comprehending coaching in all its four functions of counseling, mentoring, tutoring, and confronting. An understanding of coaching as essentially composed of two processes has enormous practical value for teaching managers to coach. The most effective and efficient way for managers to improve their coaching practices is to learn how to manage the two generic processes of solving problems and improving performance. These processes are discussed in more detail later in this book.

We know that there are some specific skills that managers use to develop the processes of successful coaching. These skills are covered in detail in the chapters on coaching processes. Many of these core skills serve to develop information.

I propose the following definition of coaching:

> Successful coaching is a mutual conversation between manager and employee that follows a predictable process and leads to superior performance, commitment to sustained improvement, and positive relationships.

Why Some "Coaching" Fails

Before proceeding, I should like to clear up a few misconceptions about coaching.

The Lack of a Process Model

In conducting seminars on coaching, I routinely hear a large number of "what if" questions, such as the following:

- "What if the employee goes off on tangents and doesn't want to discuss what I want to talk about?"
- "What if the employee is perfectly satisfied with the job and doesn't want to go any further?"
- "What if the employee doesn't ever accept the fact that there is a problem?"
- "What if the employee doesn't want to tell me why he's not focusing on the job?"

At first glance, these questions seem to be different. When, however, one begins to examine the questions in depth with managers, one finds the same underlying issue. Managers often have no way to analyze systematically what works and what does not work in coaching because they have no base line or model against which they can compare what they do. Before managers begin to learn that successful coaching follows a sequential process, they think of their coaching conversations as consisting of random inputs from themselves and their employees. Sometimes these conversations work and sometimes they do not. The managers usually do not know any more about why they worked than why they did not work.

Coaching that does not follow a specific process may sometimes succeed, but it will more often fail. Until managers discipline themselves to employ a model for coaching, they will always have an endless number of "What if?" questions. Coaching conversations that are random produce random results.

The Lack of Responsibility

In all the years that I have been teaching managers to coach, I have never had managers offer examples or anecdotes that described what *they* did wrong. Even when they talk about the difficulties that they have faced in coaching, they seem to believe that it was the employee's "fault." As one listens, one develops an image of an employee involved in a coaching conversation with no manager present.

Coaching is an interaction. What the manager does stimulates reactions in the employee. What the employee does presents the manager with alternative ways to react. Whether they admit it or not, managers influence the outcomes of every coaching session— for better or for worse. Coaching does not fail because of poorly endowed and poorly motivated employees. It can fail because of poorly trained managers.

Key Learning Points for Chapter Two

I. Coaching has four functions:

- Counseling;

- Mentoring;

- Tutoring; and

- Confronting.

II. The criteria for successful coaching are:

1. It results in a positive change in performance and a new or renewed commitment to:

    - Self-sufficiency (counseling);

    - The organization's goals and values (mentoring);

    - Continuous learning (tutoring); and

    - A sustained, high level of performance (confronting).

2. It results in achievement or maintenance of a positive work relationship.

3. It is mutual, communicates respect, and is problem-focused, change-oriented, and disciplined.

4. It follows an identifiable sequence or flow and requires the use of specific communication skills.

Chapter Three.
Coaching Process 1:
Solving Problems

C oaching Process 1, solving problems, includes the coaching functions of counseling, mentoring, and tutoring. These conversations may be initiated by the manager or the employee. These conversations may focus on teaching a technical skill, resolving an organizational problem, identifying career-development opportunities, solving personal problems, etc. All are special applications of the general process of solving problems. (This does not include those conversations that are confrontational in nature; such conversations are discussed in Chapter Four, Coaching Process 2: Improving Performance.)

Process: General Characteristics

A fundamental assumption of this book is that coaching is most likely to be successful when managers create a process. The following are the characteristics of the process.

Satisfaction: The Key to Coaching Success

A general way of describing the process is that it is a conversation that follows a flow that is logically and psychologically satisfying for the employee. It is because the process is satisfying that it works. This notion of satisfaction gives managers a new and useful way to think about their coaching conversations. It suggests that coaching must be disciplined to be successful. Managers must have sufficient discipline to create conversations that are satisfying.

Most managers that I have observed conducting coaching conversations are more likely to concentrate directly on the results they want to achieve than they are on the conversation by which these results can be achieved. They focus on the issue that the employee presents (counseling), or on communicating some "unwritten" code of behavior to the employee (mentoring), or on improving the employee's skill (tutoring), or on improving something (confronting). However, for these final outcomes to be met, the conversation itself must meet the needs of both parties—especially those of the employee.

Reaching the desired results depends on the employee's willingness to cooperate. The manager's job is to create this willingness (or at least not to diminish it) in the coaching conversation. Cooperation becomes the sufficient condition for achieving the final results of coaching. It fosters the employee's desire to find the best solutions with the manager.

Logically Satisfying

Coaching conversations are logically satisfying for employees when employees:

- Perceive that there is a serious attempt to be objective and descriptive;
- Experience an orderly progression from one point to the next; and
- Have a sense that the conversation is focused and centers on one topic or a set of closely related topics.

Objective and Descriptive. None of us feel satisfied in conversations or relationships when we sense that we are being subjected to the whims and biases of someone else. Coaching conversations will not be positive experiences for employees if these conversations are based largely on the manager's subjective perceptions and opinions or the manager's inferences about the employees' attitudes and motives.

Complete objectivity is a goal. It is unlikely that it can be fully achieved in any human enterprise, including coaching, However, it is important that the manager do everything possible to ensure that the employee does not feel that he or she has been treated in an arbitrary or "high-handed" manner.

Being objective and being descriptive are related coaching skills. Managers are objective when they reason from verifiable information. Managers are descriptive when they provide as much verifiable information as possible.

"Being objective" should be thought of as a process of creating a *reference point* during a coaching session that both manager and employee agree exists, that both understand, and that both can use in making decisions during the coaching conversation. Coaching is most objective when managers reach decisions with employees that are based on such verifiable, objective reference points as:

- Clearly defined and achievable performance standards;
- Analyses of trends in productivity and quality;
- Verifiable selection and promotion criteria;
- Specific skills and knowledge required;
- Technical requirements;
- Observed behavior;
- Organizational procedures or regulations; and
- Careful problem analysis.

The following are examples of less objective and more objective inputs that a manager might make during the four types of coaching conversations.

1. Counseling

   Less objective: So, the root of the problem is that your contract monitor makes unrealistic and arbitrary demands of you.

   More objective: So the root of the problem is that your contract monitor is asking for services that go beyond what our contract authorizes.

2. Mentoring

   Less objective: The key to getting ahead in this organization is to be a team player.

   More objective: There are two keys to getting ahead in this organization. First, be immediately responsive to any requests for help that your boss or your peers make. Second, never make others look foolish or technically incompetent in front of their peers or bosses.

3. Tutoring

   Less objective: It seems as if we are back to square one. Your last paper doesn't show that the technical-writing course has solved your problem.

   More objective: Let's go over this last paper, section by section, and compare each one to the guidelines that you learned in your technical-writing course.

4. Confronting

   Less objective: So you just were not paying attention when I told you when I wanted the report submitted.

   More objective: Somehow we missed the boat in agreeing on the date on which the report was to be submitted.

"Being descriptive" refers to the amount of verifiable information that the manager injects into a coaching conversation. Being descriptive increases the objectivity in coaching.

In counseling, managers are descriptive when they define as fully as possible all the possible causes of problems. In mentoring, managers are descriptive when they provide numerous examples to describe the special values and idiosyncracies of upper management. Managers are descriptive in tutoring when they demonstrate skills or solutions to problems. They are descriptive in confronting when they refer in detail to what can be *observed* about employee performance rather that what they infer about people's intentions or attitudes.

The examples used in the discussion of objectivity can be used again to show how being descriptive increases objectivity.

1. Counseling

   Less descriptive: So, the root of the problem is that your contract monitor is asking for services that go beyond what our contract authorizes.

   More descriptive: There seem to be two ways that your customer is exceeding authorizations in the contract. First, he is asking for extra progress reports. Second, he is asking for more meetings than the travel budget will support.

2. Mentoring

   Less descriptive: There are two keys to getting ahead in this organization. First, be immediately responsive to any requests for help that your boss or your peers make. Second, never make others look foolish or technically incompetent in front of their peers or bosses.

   More descriptive: To get ahead, it is imperative during your first few years in the company to establish yourself as a cooperative and helpful person. There are several ways to do this. First, never bring problems to your boss for which you don't have at least two proposed solutions. Second, never make more work for your boss by failing to meet deadlines. Third, always figure out some way to help your peers when they ask for help. Never turn anyone down flatly. Always do something to help—even if you can't do everything that is asked.

3. Tutoring

   Less descriptive: Let's go over this last paper, section by section, and compare each one to the guidelines that you learned in your technical-writing course.

   More descriptive: Let's review the recommended guidelines for technical papers that you learned in the course. Then I would like you to compare each section of your paper with these guidelines to see where you find opportunities for improvement. I will then review each section, and we will end up with a specific list of changes to be made.

4. Confronting

Less descriptive: Somehow we missed the boat in agreeing on the date on which the report was to be submitted.

More descriptive: We only had the one meeting to discuss the report and the due date. I walked away with one understanding and you with another. In the future, we need to take a minute at the end to ensure that we have a common understanding of key points.

Orderly Progression. Coaching conversations are most likely to be satisfying if they have a logical sequence. Tutoring conversations proceed best if what is to be learned is first identified and then each learning step is identified. Problems in a counseling session are best resolved if all the relevant information about the general problem is explored first, the general problem is then refined to a specific one, and, finally, the contributing causes for the problem are listed.

Focused. How much should be covered in any coaching conversation is determined by how much can be remembered. Coaching conversations should be focused initially by managers who decide the general function of the conversation, to counsel, to mentor, to tutor, or to confront.

Within each of these functions, the coaching conversation should be further focused on a specific topic: the one most important thing to be learned (tutoring), the one most important problem that the employee has (counseling), and so on.

Psychologically Satisfying

Coaching conversations are psychologically satisfying for employees when they:

- Perceive that they can seriously influence the outcomes of the conversation;

- Feel that their feelings are acknowledged and understood; and

- Have a sense of completeness or closure from the conversation.

Influence. Extending influence is discussed in Chapter One as a strategy for building employee commitment. In each coaching conversation, managers create the experience of influence to the degree that the conversation is truly mutual.

The experience of influence is decided by the way in which questions such as these are answered:

- Did the employee participate fully in deciding the nature of the problem (counseling)?

- Was the employee involved in researching his or her career options (mentoring)?

- Did the employee help to determine his or her learning goals and speed of instruction (tutoring)?

- Did the employee's point of view about the performance problem receive full consideration (confronting)?

The first attribute of the process is that it is a conversation that satisfies certain logical and psychological needs of the employee. Managers who want to become successful coaches must learn how to create satisfying processes with their employees in order to maximize the employees' willingness to cooperate.

Interactive

A second attribute of the process is that it is interactive. This interactive quality is implied by terms such as mutual and one-to-one. Now we will examine the behavioral aspects of interaction.

Coaching, like all interpersonal conversations, occurs through the actions of two people—acting and reacting to each other. But coaching, like all purposeful conversations, is successful to the degree that someone is consciously or intuitively managing the interaction.

Process, as the term is used here, describes a sequential interaction between a manager and an employee in which the manager initiates behavior that is useful and reacts to the employee's behavior with behavior that is useful. Coaching is behavior. What the manager *does*—not what the manager *intends* to do—is what exists for the employee. Successful coaching requires that managers become sufficiently disciplined to behave in such a way that they maximize the possibility of creating a successful process. It means

learning to use communication behaviors that have a high probability of being effective and avoiding behaviors that are not likely
to further the goals of the process.

The first two general characteristics of process are: (a) it satisfies
the logical and psychological needs of the employee; and (b) it is
a disciplined interaction that is created by the initiating behavior
and responding behavior of the manager.

Interdependent Stages

A third characteristic of a process is that it proceeds through certain identifiable stages. Each stage has its own goals. The goals of
one stage theoretically must be met before the conversation can move
to the next stage.

Coaching Process 1, solving problems, has three stages (see
Figure 3). They are:

- Involving,
- Developing, and
- Resolving.

Stages flow into one another. As managers use the process, they
sometimes will find themselves accomplishing some of the goals
in Stage I as they are moving to Stage II. They also will find
themselves moving back and forth between stages and recycling
back through the whole process. Often, for example, one will find
that the real issue surfaces just as one thinks a counseling session
is ending. Or one discovers later that an employee has missed a
point that one thought was covered in a tutoring session.

Skills

For each stage of the process, a set of special skills are listed in the
figure. These skills are particularly useful in reaching the goals of
that stage. A process is developed and furthered through each of
its dependent stages as the manager employs these skills. Skills
should be thought of as cumulative. A manager begins a coaching

session using the skills that are useful for achieving the goals of Stage I. These skills also are useful at later stages in the process.

In summary, a process is a conversation that:

- Provides a satisfying experience for employees by meeting certain logical and psychological needs;
- Is an interaction that the manager influences for better or worse;
- Moves through a series of interdependent stages; and
- Requires a set of specific communication skills.

Figure 3, Coaching Process 1: Solving Problems, is a graphic description of the process that underlies the functions of counseling, mentoring, and tutoring. It depicts a process model that was derived not from theory but from observation. As such, it provides managers with a guide on which they can rely to achieve practical results and which they can adapt to each situation in which they undertake these coaching functions.

The idea that coaching is a process is a different approach to coaching than the ones that managers typically learn. It encourages managers to concentrate on the *sequence and flow* of the conversation as much as on the content.

Process Stage I: Involving

Stage I Goals

Involving describes the initial stage of a Process 1 coaching conversation. The goals that the manager should have in mind at this stage are to:

- Clarify the purpose of the conversation—what is being discussed, what the expected outcomes are, etc.;
- Involve the employee in a free and easy interaction;
- Clarify any important ground rules or constraints such as time, confidentiality, roles and responsibilities, etc.; and
- Develop comfort and trust.

Process Stage I: Involving

Goals	Skills
Clear expectations	*Clarifying:* Establishing objectives for the coaching session.
Comfort	
Trust	*Attending:* Using nonverbal behavior to communicate; listening nonevaluatively.
	Acknowledging: Giving verbal and nonverbal indications of being involved in the conversation.
	Probing: Asking questions and directing.
	Reflecting: Stating in one's own words what the other person has said or is feeling.
	Indicating respect: Not using behaviors that ridicule, generalize, or judge.

Process Stage II: Developing

COUNSELING:

Goals	Skills
Information	*Self Disclosure:* Indicating that one has had a similar experience.
Insight	
	Immediacy: Drawing attention to what is happening in the conversation.
	Summarizing: Pausing in the conversation to summarize key points.

Figure 3. Coaching Process Model 1: Solving Problems

MENTORING AND TUTORING:

Goals	Skills
Learning	*Concreteness:* Being specific and objective in communicating information and expectations.
	Resourcing: Giving information, advice, instruction; referring.
	Confirming: Closing the loop; ensuring that information has been received and learning has occurred.

Process Stage III: Resolving

Goals	Skills
Closure	*Reviewing:* Going over key points of session to ensure common understanding.
Next steps	
Positive relationship	*Planning:* Building strategies and agreeing on next steps.
Commitment	
	Affirming: Commenting on an employee's strengths and positive prospects.

Figure 3 (continued).

Hindrances

Coaching is a mutual interaction. Managers should quickly get the employee involved in a process that the employee perceives as balanced and which he or she can influence. It helps if the manager is aware of some of the obstacles or hindrances to building such a perception.

One hindrance is an environment that suggests formality or a serious power imbalance.

> I remember once trying to discuss a project with my boss. I was having a very tough time getting commitment from the key functional managers who were supposed to provide technical support. I sat down in my boss's office. He had a flag stationed on each side of his desk. Behind him were all his diplomas and award certificates. Even as I began to try to explain my problem, I felt hopeless. How could this person possibly understand and help with a problem of such low status as mine. My boss, by the way, did not disappoint me. He neither understood nor helped. He entered a hierarchical role when he came to work and he never once departed from it.

Asking an employee to sit across from the manager's desk can inhibit a free and mutual exchange of information between the two. One way to minimize this potential problem is for both persons to sit in chairs of equal status directly facing each other. Another way is to use some area other than the manager's office, such as a table in a conference room. In such a case, it is best if the manager does *not* sit at the head of the table but sits directly across from the employee.

Another hindrance to reaching the goals of the first stage—mutuality, trust, and comfort—is for the manager to do something that intimidates the employee. This includes saying something such as, "I'm going to go over this procedure just one more time. After this, I expect you to master it on your own and I don't expect any more mistakes." What this achieves, of course, is to so anger and threaten the employee that most of the employee's energy will be taken up during the session in handling these emotions rather than in learning the procedure.

Sometimes managers ask me (especially in regard to counseling), "Is it all right to take notes?" The only person, of course, who can answer that question is the employee. If the manager starts to take notes without checking with the employee, the employee may well regard the act with suspicion or resentment. It would be wise for the manager to explain at the beginning of the session *why* he or she thinks it would be a good idea to take notes (e.g., to record information to be referred to later in order to share it with the employee, to note action items, or to review the notes with the employee at the end of the session in order to make sure that nothing was misconstrued or interpreted incorrectly).

There are other hindrances to reaching the goals of Stage I. Many of these fall into the category of not communicating respect. Keeping an employee waiting, permitting phone calls and other interruptions, placing overly strict limitations on a conversation (e.g., "We are going to discuss this topic and no other topic during the conversation")—these and many similar behaviors put the employee in a "one down" position and seriously hinder the productive generation of information. These and most other hindrances will be overcome by a serious commitment to the skills and goals of Stage I.

Stage I Skills

The critical skills for developing Stage I are:

- Clarifying,
- Attending,
- Acknowledging,
- Probing,
- Reflecting, and
- Indicating respect.

These skills also are essential for developing Stage II and can be useful throughout the entire process.

Clarifying

The manager has responsibility for establishing the objectives of the session with the employee as quickly as possible. If the employee has initiated the session, clarification may begin with a question. If the manager has initiated the conversation, clarification begins with the manager's statement. Examples are:

- "I gather that you must be having some problems with the new quality-assurance procedures. Tell me what the difficulty is" (counseling).

- "I would like to help you figure out which jobs would be best for you to go after next" (mentoring).

- "There are three key steps in the new procedure. I would like for you to be satisfied that you understand them before we finish today" (tutoring).

- "I have the feeling that you are not yet comfortable giving orders to the people who used to be your peers. If I'm right, I'd like to help in any way I can" (counseling).

Attending

Attending has two aspects:

- It conveys to the employee that the manager is listening;

- It ensures that the manager does listen.

Attending includes all behaviors that communicate to the employee that the manager is listening. These are nonverbal behaviors such as not allowing interruptions or distractions by other people or things; not doing anything that detracts from the conversation (such as making telephone calls, signing letters, etc.); facing the employee; maintaining body language that indicates openness and interest; and being animated.

> One of my past supervisors was very preoccupied with time. Whenever he asked me into his office, he invariably had me sit under a clock. Throughout the entire conversation, his head would bob up and down between my face and the clock above me. It was very distracting, to say the least. I felt that I was an imposition and that whatever time I took up was too much. Because of this, I cut short the information that I could have provided him.

The nonverbal aspects of attending do not ensure that the manager is actually listening. Establishing good eye contact, facing the employee, and so on, do not translate directly into hearing and observing what an employee is communicating. However, the nonverbal aspects of attending do *indicate* that the manager is listening, and such behaviors encourage the employee to communicate and facilitate the achievement of the Stage I goals of comfort and trust.

The first aspect of attending is that the manager conveys to the employee (by means of nonverbal behavior) that the manager is listening. The second aspect of attending is that the manager does listen. This aspect is largely a function of the manager's ability to listen nonevaluatively. This is the ability to listen without taking sides or deciding that the speaker's statement is true or false, right or wrong. It is the ability to focus on what the other person is saying and to discover the meaning in the communication.

We listen evaluatively by:

- Being too quick to answer a question, rather than trying to listen to the question;

- Forcing a problem into our own frame of reference and mind set, rather than developing enough information to determine exactly what the problem is;

- Quickly deciding that what the other person has said is right or wrong, rather than just trying to find out what the person's point of view is.

All of us probably have had the following experiences in conversations with managers who thought they were helping:

- They responded to a question that we asked by answering some other questions that we did not ask. We ended up getting information that we did not need and not getting information that we did need.

- They treated a performance problem as though we did not know how to do the job and spent time tutoring us on a procedure that we already understood. They never found out that our problem was a lack of resources or some other environmental factor.

- They asked us for our opinion about an issue, but when we gave it, they spent the next ten minutes telling us why it was wrong.

When managers listen evaluatively they respond evaluatively. The danger is that managers will quickly create blocks to the free and easy development of a mutual interaction.

It is, therefore, important that managers learn to listen *nonevaluatively.* Learning to listen nonevaluatively can be a two-step process. Learning to give nonevaluative responses encourages one to listen nonevaluatively, and learning to listen nonevaluatively increases the probability of giving nonevaluative responses.

Acknowledging

Acknowledging includes a variety of verbal responses that communicate to the employee that the manager is involved in the conversation. If one learns to give nonevaluative responses that acknowledge what the speaker has said, one is reminded to actually listen nonevaluatively. Examples of acknowledging responses are:

- Brief verbal statements such as "uh-huh," "mmmm," "I see," "O.K.," "yes," "right," or "I understand";
- Assurances such as "Yes, I can understand that," "I can see that," or "I can understand how you felt";
- Comments such as "So that's how it happened."

Acknowledging behavior stimulates the employee to continue. It furthers the development of information. It also reminds the listener not to interrupt and not to make evaluative statements or other mistakes.

Indicating Respect

Communicating respect means that the manager behaves in such a way that he or she stimulates the free and open development of information and does nothing to inhibit this development. In particular, managers should avoid the behaviors described below.

1. *Discounting.* These behaviors communicate to employees that their problems are unreal, exaggerated, or of no importance or simply belong to a general class. Examples of discounting statements are:

- "I think you're making too much of this. It can't be as bad as you think."
- "I think that time will take care of your concerns. The longer you stay with us, the easier it will get."

- "Most women seem to feel that way (make that kind of mistake, etc.)"
- "It's my job to help all my employees."

2. *Ridiculing.* These behaviors exaggerate an employee's mistakes or apparent failures.

- "Congratulations, Bob, I conclude from your behavior yesterday that you intended to find the most creative way of making the whole team look like fools to the Vice President."
- "You were as about as well organized as a busted beehive in that presentation this morning."

3. *Being judgmental.* These behaviors indicate that the employee is to blame for whatever may have happened.

- "If you thought the valve might fail, why didn't you replace it before you went home?"
- "Maybe you just haven't tried hard enough to get along with the others."
- "I think you're making too much of this. I can't believe our people have that kind of prejudice."

One quality that managers consistently develop in successful coaching conversations is respect. They use behaviors that encourage a free exchange of opinion and information. They avoid behaviors that stimulate resistance or resentment and block the free exchange of opinion and information.

The following are examples of a manager's responses to employee statements that might occur during a coaching session. Note that the responses that demonstrate respect either stimulate the development of useful information or put no obstacle in the way of such development. In contrast, the nonrespectful responses do little to develop useful information or actually encourage the development of useless information.

Employee Statement: "I don't see how I can be expected to use one computer to do my work and a second one for the new network system."

Nonrespectful Response #1: "Everyone seems to have that sort of problem with the new system" (discounting).

Nonrespectful Response #2: "How is it that other people seem to be able to make the system work and use two computers?" (judgmental).

Respectful Response: "What are the specific kinds of problems that you have?" (open probe).

Employee Statement: "I can't work with the new operator. It's easier to do the job than to try to teach him. I just don't have the time."

Nonrespectful Response #1: "You'll have to find time. Training operators is part of your job" (discounting).

Nonrespectful Response #2: "Nobody finds it easy. All our people have the same problem" (discounting).

Nonrespectful Response #3: "Yeh, I know just about where you put training operators—somewhere after lunch and golf" (ridiculing).

Respectful Response: "Let's review your work priorities and see exactly where the major conflicts exist" (open probe).

Employee Statement: "I thought I understood your priorities on safety training and that you really meant for all my people to complete the new course before the end of the year."

Nonrespectful Response #1: I thought that you would make a sensible judgment to keep training from interfering with production. But obviously you didn't" (judgmental).

Nonrespectful Response #2: "I think you just lost sight of why we are in business. Our job isn't to train, it's to produce cars" (judgmental).

Respectful Response: "I can see how we could have failed to connect on this. Let's see how we can keep the critical numbers on the floor and still get the people trained" (acknowledging, open probe).

Probing

This skill refers to those behaviors that request or direct. During coaching sessions, managers may request information with questions or they may politely direct employees to give information.

There is little difference between "Please tell me what happened" and "Can you tell me what happened?"

Closed probes encourage "yes" or "no" responses or short responses with a single-item content. Examples of these are:

- "How much money is left in the budget?"
- "Which directive did you apply in this case?"
- "Tell me the most important new skill that you want to learn."
- "Have you discussed this with your lead person?"

Open probes encourage elaboration. Examples of these are:

- "Tell me how you are getting on with the project."
- "Tell me how you decided which of the directives applied."
- "What are your general career expectations at this point?"

A few points are worth remembering concerning the use of open and closed probes. First, the purpose of all probes is to develop information. The use of open probes is like going fishing with a net; you catch a number of fish. Closed probes are like fishing with a hook; you are trying to catch one fish at a time. If one is trying to gather as much information as possible from an employee, open probes usually help. However, if one is focusing on a specific issue, trying to eliminate alternatives, or testing for concurrence, closed probes are more useful.

A second point is that closed probes are not always responded to as closed probes. The question "Do you have sufficient resources to complete the project?" is in the form of a closed probe, but if asked such a question, an employee would most likely give an extensive description of what resources were still needed to finish the project. One cannot predict how another person will respond to any probe.

A third point is a note of caution. As I have watched managers conducting coaching conversation, I have observed their strong bias for closed probes. Sometimes the so-called coaching conversations resemble interrogations or diagnostic interviews. When they are strung together, without any encouragement to the employee to elaborate, closed probes can convey very strongly that the manager is in control of the conversation. What often results is that the employee becomes passive and just waits to respond to the next closed question.

Reflecting

Reflecting responses briefly restate what the employee has said (content) or what the employee is feeling (emotions). This technique is also called "mirroring" and "active listening." Such responses communicate understanding and encourage the development of information. Some examples of employee statements and reflecting

Statement: "I don't really understand what top management wants. They say our order of priorities is safety, quality, and schedule. But just let it look like a test is going to slip a day and all hell breaks loose."

Response: "It seems to you that you are getting mixed messages, and it still looks to you as if schedule is number one."

Statement: "With all these changes hitting us at once, my group is in mass confusion. I'm sure tired of telling my people that I don't know any more than they do."

Response: "From where you sit, it feels like there are no answers to anything right now, just questions."

Statement: "All they do for supervisors is tell us what we can't do. We've got about as much power over our employees as I have over the weather."

Response: "You're expected to get the same amount of work out of your people, but with less and less clout."

Reflecting is not a skill that comes naturally to most people, but it is particularly useful in coaching and is a valuable skill in most other managerial conversations. Some of the reasons why reflecting is such an effective communication skill are as follows:

1. To reflect, you must listen. Reflecting forces and focuses listening; it builds better listening skills. You cannot restate or convey understanding of an employee's feelings unless you have heard accurately what the employee has said.

2. The value of reflecting responses is that they develop information even when they are not quite accurate or on target. When a reflecting response is off target, the employee almost always will clarify what she or he has said.

The preceding discussions have covered the skills that are useful in reaching the goals of Stage I. However, these skills have continued utility throughout the entire coaching process.

Process Stage II: Developing

Stage II Goals

Stage II of Coaching Process 1, solving problems, will vary according to the specific function of the coaching conversation. If it is a counseling conversation, the emphasis in Stage II is on developing information that leads to problem definition and employee understanding of and *insight* into the problem. If the function is mentoring, the purpose of Stage II is that the employee *learn* from the manager's advice about such things as company politics, company culture, and career patterns. If the coaching function is tutoring, Stage II focuses on *learning* from instruction.

Managers who do successful coaching use all the skills identified in the problem-solving process, whether the function is counseling, mentoring, or tutoring. However, each of these functions tends to employ certain skills with special frequency. The following discussion will emphasize the special utility of each skill for each function, but all the skills are used in all coaching functions.

Stage II Skills for Counseling

The goals of a counseling session in Stage II are to develop sufficient information to identify the problem accurately and to help the employee and the manager to gain insight about the problem. The skills of attending, acknowledging, probing, and reflecting (described in Stage I) are particularly useful for developing information and understanding, and three additional skills are useful at this stage. They are self-disclosure, immediacy, and summarizing.

Self-Disclosure

A manager can make certain types of statements to communicate that he or she has had an experience similar to the one that the employee is describing. Such statements tend to encourage people to feel that the listener can identify with their problem. Examples are as follows:

- "I've felt like that";
- "A similar thing happened to me";
- "My first project ran into a similar problem."

Immediacy

During a coaching conversation, a number of things can occur that keep the conversation from progressing to a positive conclusion. These include:

- The employee displays outbursts of strong emotions such as anger, hostility, fear, or anxiety;
- The employee makes little or no verbal response and behaves in a withdrawn or disinterested manner;
- The conversation becomes bogged down, going over the same ground without moving ahead;
- The employee is surprised by the topic and needs time to prepare for the discussion;
- The employee is too tired or too distracted to engage in a useful conversation.

Immediacy is the skill of responding to "real time" conditions such as those listed above. It is the skill of focusing the coaching conversation on the here and now. It includes any comment that draws *immediate* attention to anything that could block the progress of the coaching session.

One common block is that the employee is not ready for a coaching session. Just because a manager decides to have a coaching session with an employee does not mean that the time is also right for the employee. An employee who is not ready may act confused or uninvolved. Managers should not attempt to conduct coaching sessions until they have tested for employee readiness and determined whether the conversations are likely to be profitable.

During coaching, some employees may become hostile, angry, or belligerent, and managers cannot afford to ignore these emotions and behaviors. The manager should comment on what is occurring, ask whether the employee wants to continue the conversation, and reach some agreement with the employee about how to proceed.

> I once observed a manager conducting a coaching session with a subordinate. The manager was trying to get the subordinate to provide more technical direction on a project that the subordinate was leading. The two kept going around and around without reaching a solution. The manager's perspective was that the employee knew more about the project's technology than anyone else. The subordinate's position was that his job was to manage several projects and that he could not become too involved in the technology of any one project. Finally, the manager employed the skill of immediacy and said, "Look, we're not getting anywhere. All we are doing is restating our positions. This project is in technical trouble. I need your help. How about thinking about the problem—what you want and what I need—and then getting together again tomorrow to see if we can't find a solution."

Immediacy means not only drawing attention to blocks that develop during coaching conversations, it also means offering strategies for overcoming these blocks. Such strategies may include:

- Deferring the conversation to a later time;
- Pausing for a moment while the employee collects his or her thoughts;
- Trying a new tack, approaching the problem from a new angle;
- Acknowledging that both the manager and employee must compromise.

The following are a few examples of what the skill of immediacy sounds like:

- "You are clearly very angry right now. Maybe we should talk about why that is happening before we do anything else."

- "I want to fix this problem with the contractor. You seem to want to talk about your disappointment in not being promoted. I would like to talk about your disappointment, but I also need to talk about the contractor. How would you like to handle the two?"

- "I think we've started going over the same ground again. Maybe we have exhausted all the reasons why the schedule has slipped. Let's go on now and talk about how to fix the problem."

- "This subject seems to have caught you by surprise. Do you want to continue now or wait until you've had some time to think about it?"

Summarizing

A good coaching technique is to stop the development of information periodically and summarize what has been said. This helps both managers and employees to keep the key facts before them and to ensure that the conversation progresses with mutual understanding.

Examples of summarizing are:

- "A sudden increase in your work load, your losing your best lead person, and a confusion about priorities seem to be the major reasons why we've fallen behind schedule. Is that about it?"

- "Let me see if I've got this right. You've had difficulty moving into the new spaces because: one, the customer-service people didn't get out on time; two, the modification specifications were changed at the last minute; and, three, you've had trouble scheduling the down time with your customers."

Stage II Skills for Mentoring and Tutoring

The goals of mentoring and tutoring are various kinds of learning. As we observe the learning process in coaching, it proceeds like this:

1. The manager checks to make sure that the employee knows what the learning goal is, e.g., what kind of characteristics the company values in a senior executive (mentoring) or how to improve a report (tutoring).

2. The manager proceeds to advise, instruct, or demonstrate.

3. The employee shows in some way that he or she understands and can use the knowledge or skill presented by the manager.

4. The manager corrects any misconceptions or adjusts the employee's learning.

Three skills are useful in Stage II of a mentoring or tutoring conversation: concreteness, resourcing, and confirming.

Concreteness

The manager must communicate what he or she wants the employee to know or be able to do. Advising an employee that "our most successful managers are known as team players" is not specific enough to be useful to the employee. Telling an employee that his or her reports need more "punch" does not tell the employee what to do with them.

> I listened in amazement once while a general manager told one of his direct reports that he "needed to be a more professional manager," that he should "start thinking like a manager," and that he did not seem to know what "his role as a manager was." The conversation never got any more concrete than that. Yet the employee kept acknowledging agreement and left the session with no more direction than he already had.
>
> I often heard managers in the project office of an aerospace engineering firm tell their engineers—especially the new ones—that they had to be self starters in order to succeed. Some of these engineers figured

out what "self starter" meant by trial and error. Others were fired or transferred because they did not get it just right and were accused of "taking too much individual initiative."

In another firm, I had the chance to monitor a number of coaching sessions conducted by middle managers. In a mentoring session, one manager advised a subordinate supervisor that the way to get ahead was "always be a good employee and support your boss; offer some good ideas, but not too many; and learn to use good viewgraphs with your presentations." The only concrete part of this advice was the most trivial: use good viewgraphs. But the question remains: What is a good viewgraph?

Resourcing

The practice of coaching assumes that the manager is a potential source of help. Successful coaching (especially counseling, mentoring, and tutoring) rests on the assumption that managers have special knowledge and experience—unique resources—to be used in developing employees. Such resources may be:

- Information,
- Advice,
- Instruction,
- Demonstration, or
- Referral.

There are two characteristics of resourcing that require some elaboration.

- Resourcing should not preempt employee initiative or create overdependence; and
- Resourcing should always be concrete.

Dependence. The strength of coaching is that managers are potential resources. But this very fact can also be a weakness in coaching. Managers, by the nature of their jobs, are problem solvers. The danger in coaching is that managers will solve problems for their employees when they should not.

No manager should want employees who are overly dependent, who lack initiative, or who never have new ideas. Every time a manager has a coaching conversation with an employee, the manager, to some degree, must make a choice. Will the manager provide the employee an opportunity to solve the problem or will the manager solve the problem? Will the manager give the employee the opportunity to discover information or will the manager encourage the employee to become more and more dependent on the manager for information? Every time a manager resolves a problem for an employee, the manager is missing an opportunity to develop the competence of the employee. In today's jargon, this is called "disempowerment." It is the opposite of the development of competence and influence that are the keys for building employee commitment.

I am not suggesting that managers should not answer questions or solve problems, but I am cautioning managers against inadvertently encouraging dependence rather than independence in their employees.

Confirming

Managers never can be sure that information has been received and understood or that insight and learning have occurred until "the loop is closed." Confirming is a feedback skill. There are many ways in which a manager can confirm that results have been achieved.

The manager may request the employee to replay or restate what the manager has said. For example:

- "How about going over these steps in your own words and telling me how you will proceed."

- "What do you see now as the key points that should be covered in your next status review?"

A manager may confirm that information has been received or that learning has occurred by asking the employee to demonstrate some skill—either during a coaching session or later. For example:

- "How about changing the conclusion of the report—following the guidelines that we have agreed on—and getting back to me tomorrow?"

- "Here is a request for a proposal. Based on what I've been saying, what do you see that's wrong?"
- "How about giving me a practice run through tomorrow on this presentation and including all the changes that we have agreed on."

Concreteness, resourcing, and confirming are skills that have special usefulness for the functions of mentoring and tutoring. However, as is the case with all the skills included in Coaching Process 1, solving problems, these skills are applied at various times in all coaching functions.

Process Stage III: Resolving

Stage III Goals

The general and overarching goals of coaching are to obtain employee commitment to higher levels of performance while maintaining positive work relationships between managers and employees. The entire process leads toward these goals and it is through the entire process that they are achieved.

Positive relationships are developed, maintained, and strengthened by adhering to the fundamental characteristics of successful coaching such as communicating respect, ensuring that the conversation is mutual, focusing on the problem, and staying future oriented. Commitment is built throughout the conversation as the manager develops clarity, builds competence, extends influence, and expresses appreciation.

One purpose of Stage III, resolving, is to reinforce the general results of positive relationship and commitment. Two additional goals are to achieve *closure* and to plan the *next steps*.

Closure is the process of completing the coaching conversation. The goal is to reinforce the employee's sense of achievement. Closure is effected by reviewing what has transpired during the coaching conversation and by affirming the employee's current and future achievement.

Planning next steps can take a number of different forms, depending on the coaching function. In the case of counseling, the employee and manager will identify strategies for the employee to use to resolve the problems identified in Stage II. If the function is mentoring, the next steps may be for the employee to test what has been covered and then for manager and employee to have a follow-up conversation. In the case of tutoring, the next steps may be for the employee to practice the new learning or to work on additional learning projects on his or her own.

Stage III Skills

Three skills have special relevance in achieving closure and planning next steps in order to ensure that the general goals of commitment and positive relationship are reached. These skills are reviewing, planning, and affirming.

Reviewing

Developing information and learning are achievements in which the employee has participated. The primary information and learning points should be reviewed as a way of checking common understanding between the manager and employee and as a way of emphasizing the employee's achievement. Reviewing builds a sense of completeness and closure. It also encourages a visible display of the employee's commitment. Reviewing may take such forms as the following:

- "I think you have done a good job identifying the main reasons why we are behind in getting the new proposal out. See if this is correct. We didn't get clarification on the Request for Proposal until two weeks after we requested it. The new cost-estimate software turned out to have some pretty severe bugs. And your team hasn't had a chance to jell because of so many personnel changes" (counseling).
- "I think we've pretty well got our strategy together for your meeting with the Personnel Advisory Committee. First, try not to be the first person who attacks the new time-card policy. This is the general manager's own idea, and it's not in our best interest to be identified as the "bad guy." Second, make

sure that you comment on the positive features of the policy. Third, make sure that you show how the changes we want are primarily ways of cutting down on paperwork" (mentoring).

- "Now that we have covered the sections that must be included in our technical reviews, I want to go over them again so that you know exactly what the sequence is. First, include on the cover page a synopsis of what you did, your findings, and your recommendations. Second, the body of the review must include three sections: (a) a statement of the purpose of the review; (b) a description of how the paper was reviewed and references to similar published data; and (c) a statement of your conclusions with all the support you can give. If your findings are inconclusive, add a fourth section in which you state clearly why they are inconclusive" (tutoring).

Planning

In the final stage of a coaching conversation, the manager plans with the employee such things as:

- Strategies to resolve the problems identified (counseling);
- Ways to test or build on the employee's understanding of the company's culture, the values and biases of senior management, etc. (mentoring); and
- Ways to test new learning or opportunities for additional learning (tutoring).

Planning can be as simple as having an employee try out specific new learning and then report back to the manager. It can be as complicated as having an employee prepare a five- or ten-year career-development plan. It can be as impersonal as putting together a revised project schedule or as personal as deciding just how the employee will use the organization's employee-assistance program to help with a family problem.

Whatever their content or complexity, good plans tend to have the following characteristics:

- They are developed with full employee involvement (i.e., influence). The employee assumes responsibility for the plan because (to the greatest degree possible) it reflects the employee's own input and decisions.

- They are concrete, action steps. They do more than convey an intention to "try harder" or "be more sensitive" or "pay more attention to senior managers."

- They include a specific means of measuring their progress and success at a particular time in the future.

The following are some examples of partial planning conversations:

- "Well, I suggest that you try your new approach with John— giving him more latitude in the sequence than he uses in handling applications—and see how it goes for a week. Then get back to me about how it's going" (counseling).

- "After you've had a chance to find out from our rate clerks exactly what they do, what they like, and what they don't like, we can discuss whether you want to make that move. Let's plan for you to do this and get back to me no later than ten days from now" (mentoring).

- "You've got a good handle now on the steps for preparing the model. If you think that you are ready to start working on the sensors we use, find out all you can between now and Monday, O.K.?" (tutoring).

Affirming

The first general goal of successful coaching is the employee's commitment to higher levels of performance. Commitment results from two prior conditions: competence and influence. Affirming is a skill that reinforces an employee's feeling of competence. In every successful coaching conversation, employees demonstrate different kinds of new competencies. The skill of affirming draws explicit attention to these competencies. Some examples are:

- "I know it wasn't easy for you to dig into the causes for the team's performance this quarter, but you've done a fine job of analysis. I also want to commend you for the way you've accepted your share of the responsibility. I can do my job only so long as I have people like you who don't make excuses and who aren't afraid to take some heat. Thanks for helping us find a light at the end of the tunnel" (counseling).

- "You're really getting a feel for what makes this division work. Researchers are a funny lot, and you're clearly getting a handle on what makes them tick" (mentoring).

- "I think you're well over the toughest part of this new procurement sequence. You've gotten through it faster than I did" (tutoring).

Summary of Coaching Process 1: Solving Problems

The key points to remember about the process and skills for the problem-solving coaching process are as follows:

1. Coaching Process 1 describes what typically goes on in those successful coaching conversations that have the functions of counseling, mentoring, or tutoring.

2. Coaching Process 1 has three stages:

- Stage I: Involving,
- Stage II: Developing, and
- Stage III: Resolving.

3. The general flow of the process is the same, regardless of the function, but each function has its own special goals and skills. These special goals and skills are particularly evident in Stage II, developing.

4. All stages of the process are interdependent, and there typically is movement back and forth between the stages. However, the process is directional; it does move toward specific results and closure.

5. Certain stages require the use of certain skills, but most of the skills—especially the information-developing skills of Stage I—are used throughout the process.

6. It is the *process* of the coaching conversation and not the content that leads to a commitment to higher performance while maintaining a positive work relationship between manager and employee.

It is the total coaching conversation that produces the desired results most consistently. To be competent coaches, managers must be able to carry the process through from beginning to end. To illustrate Process 1 in its entirety, the next three sections of this chapter will contain examples of the three coaching functions (counseling, mentoring, and tutoring) that employ Coaching Process 1.

Examples of Coaching Process 1: Solving Problems

In the examples that follow, **M** is the symbol for manager, and **S** is the symbol for subordinate. The subordinate may be a supervisor or a nonsupervisor.

For each example, the column on the left contains the coaching conversation. The stages and skills of the process are identified in the column on the right. Stages are in boldface, and skills are in Italic. Not all skills are illustrated in each example because not all skills would always be used in any specific coaching conversation. Over the three examples, however, all the skills essential for Process 1 are presented.

How To Use the Examples

The examples are intended to serve as models that integrate and illustrate the goals, stages, and skills for the three coaching functions of counseling, mentoring, and tutoring. These models can be powerful learning tools. The following approach is suggested:

1. Before you read through an example, review Process 1 and the special skills associated with the function that the example illustrates (Figure 1);

2. Cover up the right-hand column of the example and test your ability to identify the stages and skills;

3. After you have gone through an example once, read through the example again and substitute your own responses for the ones the manager makes in the example.

Counseling: An Example

Counseling is a problem-solving conversation that may be initiated by a manager or subordinate. Some of the specific outcomes that counseling may achieve are:

- Accurate descriptions of problems and their causes;
- Technical and organizational insight;
- Venting of strong feelings;
- Changes in points of view;
- Commitment to self-sufficiency; and
- Deeper personal insight about one's feelings and behavior.

In addition, there are the general coaching outcomes of commitment and a positive work relationship.

Counseling Conversation	Comments
S: Thanks for seeing me on such short notice. I've run into a couple of problems that could delay installing the new office network and I wanted to let you know and see what you thought I might do.	**Stage I: Involving** Coaching initiated by subordinate
M: I've got a meeting in twenty minutes. Let's see how far we can get. We'll pick it up later if we have to. What's happening?	*Structuring* **Stage II: Developing** *Probing*

S: We thought we had the issue of compatibility covered. The contractor has just informed me that any hardware earlier than PC-3 won't handle the new graphics software. We have ten units that would have to be replaced.

M: So the contractor has hit you out of the blue with this one.

Reflecting

S: Right. He says that our older hardware normally would work, but that we modified it for our time-share requirements when we put it in. We failed to tell him this, so he's saying we messed up.

M: O.K., we've got a problem with the contractor and with compatibility. Is this the only holdup?

Summarizing

Closed Probe, but responded to as open

S: Well, there is a related problem. We told all the secretaries that they could use their current machines and could selectively learn the new graphics system. If what the contractor is telling me is true, I'm between a rock and a hard place with them.

M: Are those all the pieces to the puzzle?

Closed Probe

S: Yes.

M: So what we're looking at is the following: one, the contractor has told us that our older hardware

Summarizing

won't handle the graphics system.
Two, we sold the new network to the
secretaries by assuring them that they
could keep their current machines.
Third, we also told them that they
could continue to use the old
graphics package and learn the new
one over time, that both systems
would work in the new network.

S: That's about it.

M: So, how do you think we ought
to proceed?

Stage III: Resolving
Open Probe

S: I think that the acceptance of the
new network is critical. I'd like to do
everything possible before we decide
that changing from the old PCs is in-
evitable. It's been hard enough bring-
ing the secretaries with us this far. I'd
like to get at least one more opinion.
The trouble is that we already have
Netcom under contract to do the
job. If we get another opinion and
find out that Netcom was wrong,
then what?

M: I think that's the way to go.
Netcom will not want to show up as
incompetent in this. If the contractor
is wrong, I can tell you from past experience that Netcom will be glad to
renegotiate the contract. They can't
afford to look like dummies. If it
turns out that he is right, we will
have to look at our alternatives. Go
ahead and get the second opinion
but start working on your backup
plan—assuming that Netcom is right.

Resourcing

Planning

S: I'll get on it right away.

M: Thanks for keeping me in the loop. I think you've got a clear picture of what our options are. If we're lucky, Netcom is wrong. If not, I know you'll figure out some tradeoffs with the secretaries.	*Affirming*

Mentoring: An Example

Mentoring is a coaching conversation that may be initiated by the employee or the manager. It results in information that permits employees to further their own success. Mentoring can be sage advice that unlocks organizational mysteries. It is a process of sharing with employees the insights that managers have gained from personal experience. Mentoring permits employees to avoid pitfalls, to plan their careers, and to adjust their behaviors to fit organizational norms. Typical outcomes of mentoring are:

- Development of political savvy;
- Sensitivity to an organization's culture;
- Personal networking;
- Greater proactivity in managing one's career;
- Commitment to the organization's goals and values; and
- Sensitivity to the preferences of senior managers.

Mentoring Conversation	**Comments**
M: Joanne, next month you'll be giving the weekly status reports to the director. I know that you've observed me doing it, but I thought it would help if I gave you my sense of what the director likes and what seems to annoy him.	**Stage I: Involving**

S: That would help a lot. I've noticed that sometimes he's all smiles and other times he gives the presenters a pretty rough time.

M: Let's start with what he likes. First, make sure that the presentation tracks. He wants everything you say about the project to relate to what he got at the last presentation. He's got a really good memory and he does his homework.

Stage II: Developing

Resourcing

S: Should I go back further than the last presentation?

M: Only if there is a negative trend. If the project is on target, he wants minimum information. But if there is a problem, he wants to go back to the time it began. So, you've got number one on his list of likes?

Resourcing

Confirming

S: I think so. Give him backup at least one presentation deep and cover problems from the time they started.

M: Right. The second things he likes are your conclusions and your recommendations. He expects you to tell him what to do. Don't be bashful. But you had better know the science and technology that you are talking about in the smallest detail. He has no tolerance for managers who are technically stupid. So that's number two of his likes. Why don't you summarize what I've said.

Acknowledging
Resourcing

Confirming

S: One, he wants what we tell to be compared to the previous presentation and he wants the whole review on problems until they are fixed. Second, he wants me to tell him what to do, if there are decisions to be made. But I had better have the details at my fingertips.

M: Right, you've got that. Is there anything you are unclear about up to this point?

Acknowledging

Confirming

S: Just one thing. What kinds of problems do we give him?

M: Only those that will cause the schedule to slip and anything that looks like a safety hazard. Now let's look at the things that annoy him. There are really only two. The first is never, never, be late. He has a compulsion about being on time. He will never keep you waiting. Don't keep him waiting. Always have a backup presenter standing by. Second, don't try to impress him with pretty slides. Keep them clean and simple. Now let's review what we've gone over. His likes are: one, compare this week's data with last week's, but cover problems since their beginning. Two, always tell him what to do, but know every detail of what you are recommending. His pet peeves are: one, don't be late, and two, don't blow smoke with pretty slides. Keep them lean and mean. I'd like for you to think about what

Resourcing

Resourcing

Stage III: Resolving
Reviewing

Planning

we've gone over. Get back to me
on Friday. We'll review your first
presentation to see how well you've
picked up the director's likes and
dislikes.

S: That will be a big help. I sure
don't want to blow the first one.

M: If I didn't think you would do a   *Affirming*
superior job, you wouldn't be doing
it. You're as good on your feet as
anyone in the group.

S: Well, thanks for the vote of
confidence—and the help.

Tutoring: An Example

Tutoring is one-to-one teaching. It may be initiated by the manager
or the employee. Tutoring always is a supplemental process; it does
not take the place of classroom or on-the-job instruction. It is too
time consuming and intensive to replace regular, ongoing, training and development activities. It should always be focused on learning that has immediate impact on the way in which a job is per-
formed (i.e., not on skills that the employee may apply someday).

Even though tutoring has a strong orientation to the present,
it shares with all coaching functions the goal of long-term commitment. In the case of tutoring, the commitment is by employees to
their own learning. Typical examples of outcomes from tutoring conversations are:

- Increased technical competence;
- Increased breadth of technical understanding;
- Movement to expert status;
- Increased learning pace; and
- Commitment to continual learning.

Tutoring Conversation	Comments
M: You've had your first run through doing performance appraisals. I'd like to know if there is any way I can help you to make the system work better for you. I suspect that there may be one or two things that you would like to discuss or have clarified.	**Stage I: Involving** *Structuring* *Open Probe*
S: Well, I knew it wouldn't be easy, and it wasn't.	
M: For what it's worth, I think it's always been one of my toughest jobs. I learn something new each time I go through a cycle. Tell me what you found to be the most difficult part of the process.	*Self-Disclosure* *Open Probe*
S: Well, I went through all the steps that we discussed earlier. Things went quite well with my first two reviews. But I really had a problem with Gary. He was riled up before we started. He began by telling me that he's never been evaluated fairly and that this time wouldn't be any different. I ended up getting pretty angry myself. I just shouted him down at one point, put the appraisal in front of him, and told him to read it—that it was as fair as I could make it.	
M: Sounds like Gary gave you a pretty rough introduction to the process.	*Reflecting*

S: Yeah, he really made my day. I actually had a lot of very positive feedback that I wanted to give him, but
we never got to it. Now I wonder if
I was too good to him on the
appraisal.

M: So you lost your cool. As you   *Reflecting*
think about it now, what do you im-   *Open Probe*
agine you could have done—or
would like to have done—differently?

S: I guess I should have calmed him
down somehow, or set the meeting
up differently. But, honestly, I don't
know what I could have done very
differently.

M: Let me try a couple of ideas on   **Stage II: Developing**
you. First, for whatever reason, Gary
sure wasn't ready to have a
performance-appraisal session. So,
one alternative would be to put it off
for a day to give him a chance to   *Resourcing*
cool down.

S: Right. I just let the conversation
get out of hand because I was so
completely taken by surprise.

M: Another alternative would be   *Resourcing*
to forget about the appraisal and
use the session to find out what
was bothering Gary.

S: I could have done that. I was just
programmed to get those appraisals
out of the way, and I couldn't get off
my own agenda.

M: A third strategy might be to check with Gary—and all your employees—some time before their appraisals to make sure that it is a good time for them. All of us have crises come up, and facing an appraisal may be the last straw—even though it's been scheduled. I think the more control over these things you can give your employees, the better.

Resourcing

S: Thanks. I'll try to slow down and think of alternatives next time. It looks like anything can happen in an appraisal session.

M: Did you have any other questions or concerns?

Open Probe

S: No, none that I can think of.

M: O.K., then tell me what—in hindsight—you think your alternatives with Gary might have been.

Confirming and Reviewing

S: Well, I could have called time out and told him I would reschedule the meeting; or just forgotten about the appraisal for the time being and found out what was bothering him; or checked with him earlier in the day to see if our scheduled time was still good for him.

M: I think that you've learned a lot lot from this one experience. Don't forget that the others went well. I suspect that you will respond to

Affirming

anyone who pulls a "Gary" on you
in the future with a lot more savvy.

Key Learning Points for Chapter Three

There are certain general characteristics of all successful coaching processes:

- Employees experience the process as satisfying their logical and psychological needs;
- The processes are interactive and are created by the behaviors that managers use to initiate them and to respond;
- Coaching processes have interdependent stages; the goals of one stage must be met before the goals of the following stage can be;
- Coaching processes are created and made useful by the disciplined use of specific communication skills.

The three stages and goals of Coaching Process 1, solving problems, are as follows:

- Stage I: Involving: Clear expectations, comfort, and trust.
- Stage II: Developing: Information, insight, and learning.
- Stage III: Resolving: Closure, next steps, positive relationship, and commitment.

Chapter Four.
Coaching Process 2:
Improving Performance

The coaching conversation that is intended to improve performance is *confronting.* The short-term goal of confronting is to make an immediate, positive adjustment in an employee's performance. The manager may want an employee to perform some task at a satisfactory level, e.g., to keep accurate records or to submit a report in proper form; or the manager may want to move an employee from a satisfactory level to a superior level of performance; or the manager may hope to move an employee into tasks that are more difficult and complex, e.g., from doing data collection to doing statistical analysis.

It is, of course, more difficult for managers to convey to employees that they want them to move from an unsatisfactory to a satisfactory level than it is for them to indicate that they want the employees to move to a higher level. The latter usually is viewed by employees quite positively—even as a compliment. However, telling employees that they are not performing at a satisfactory level is perceived as a reprimand. Much of the material in this chapter will focus on the more difficult type of coaching conversation: confronting less-than-satisfactory performance. If managers master the more difficult conversation, they will be able to perform the less difficult one.

Before discussing the process itself, it may be wise to make a distinction between confrontation and criticism and to describe the ways in which confrontation can be made more difficult than it need be.

Confrontation and Criticism

Confrontation is a coaching process by which managers correct performance problems, develop commitment to continual improvement, and maintain positive relationships with employees. In the context of coaching, it means to face problems squarely and deal with them, not to face them defiantly or antagonistically. It is a skilled and disciplined process of presenting the problem and managing performance. Confrontation is not criticism; in fact, criticism is counterproductive. The differences between confrontation and criticism are displayed in Figure 4.

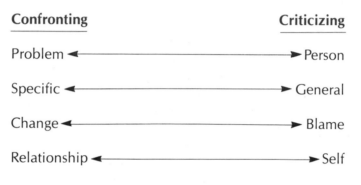

Confronting	**Criticizing**
Problem ◄──────────────────►	Person
Specific ◄──────────────────►	General
Change ◄──────────────────►	Blame
Relationship ◄──────────────────►	Self

Figure 4. Confrontation Versus Criticism

Problem Versus Person

Confrontation focuses on a specific performance problem. It identifies concretely an improvement that the manager wants. It describes an expectation that can be understood by the employee. Confrontation is objective.

A few examples of positive confrontation are:

- "Your budget was due yesterday. When will it be ready?"

- "Telling the vice president at the meeting this morning that she didn't have her facts right clearly annoyed her and didn't help our cause much. I'd like to figure out a strategy with you that protects your integrity without encouraging hostility from the top."

Criticism, on the other hand, focuses on the personal characteristics of employees—their attitudes and personal traits. Examples are:

- "You obviously don't take any pride in your work anymore."
- "What's happened to your motivation? It looks like you've retired on the job."

Specific Versus General

Confrontation identifies precisely what the manager thinks should occur or change. Even when the problem may be a recurring one, confrontation starts with the most recent example of the undesired performance. Examples are:

- "Your time card shows that you have been late four out of the last six work days. I expect you to be here by eight."
- "I haven't received your revised timetable for the move. I need it no later than tomorrow so I can coordinate the whole department's move."

Criticism tends to be general. It often magnifies a single error or mistake with the use of words such as "always," "never," "typically," and "continually." The following are some examples of criticism.

- "You never try to go the extra mile. You always put yourself before the interests of the team."
- "You persist in not doing it right. No matter how many times I tell you, you just keep on doing it your way."

Change Versus Blame

Confrontation is designed to effect improvement. Managers who know how to confront are clearly focused on the desired change in performance. They are not interested in apologies or guilt. They do not want their employees to feel weak or pessimistic. They want the employees to decide to improve and to believe that they *can* improve. Confrontation, therefore, always focuses on what can be changed: the future.

Criticism, on the other hand, establishes blame. Managers who criticize expect employees to feel guilty for their mistakes. Criticism focuses on what cannot be changed: the past.

- "You demonstrated a lack of sensitivity in being late for our meeting this morning. It has caused me and your colleagues a lot of embarrassment. How could you do such a thing?" (criticism).

- "You were late for our meeting this morning. I can't complete the process without you. I would like to know how we can keep this from happening again" (confrontation).

- "Why did you leave the machine on last night? What do you have to do that's so important that you can't take time to shut it off?" (criticism).

- "I noticed that the machine was still on this morning when I came in. The log indicates that you were the last one to leave. I'd like to figure out a way to make sure that the machine is turned off each evening" (confrontation).

Relationship Versus Self

The purpose of coaching for commitment is to improve performance, increase commitment, and maintain a positive work relationship. Maintaining a positive relationship is a primary focus in confrontation, and confrontation can put this relationship at higher risk than can the other coaching functions. This focus is different from the focus of criticism, which centers only on the needs of the person doing the criticizing. Criticism is often done in anger, largely to allow the criticizer to vent his or her feelings.

Added Difficulties

Confronting is not easy. All coaching conversations (especially confronting) require that managers be skilled and disciplined in creating and using the processes. However, people can make confronting a performance problem more difficult than it needs to be. Some of the ways in which we do this are as follows.

1. We avoid confronting problems as long as possible, so that, when we do confront them, it is a strategy of last resort.

2. We fail to establish clear performance standards that permit employees to manage their own performance.

3. We fail to give timely, sufficient feedback to enable employees to adjust their performance to meet managers' expectations.

4. We fail to express sufficient, uncontaminated appreciation for positive achievement.

Avoidance

Confronting performance problems is an experience that many managers would like to avoid.

> A bank president once contacted me about conducting training in interpersonal relations and communications for his senior staff. When we met, he confided that he planned to retire in two years and that the board and he had decided that Gerald would take his place. Gerald was extremely competent, probably the best loan manager that the bank had ever had, and he knew the bank's operation from top to bottom. However, many of the bank's clients were farmers, and Gerald seemed to offend them. There were complaints from time to time that he was insensitive. The president of the bank did not want to hurt Gerald's feelings or single him out as the one person who needed the training, so he was prepared to contract for training for all the senior people!

Few managers resort to this extreme to avoid confrontation, but too many managers do avoid timely confrontation. They avoid it because it stimulates negative emotions, and they believe that negative emotions threaten their work relationships with their employees.

When people are confronted, they usually feel that they are under attack. The most typical responses to verbal attack are: (a) to become passive and withdraw; (b) to make excuses and rationalize; and (c) to take the offensive and strike back. Typical employee responses are to cry (passive); to just sit there looking sullen or depressed (passive); to say how hard they are trying and how impossible the job is (excuses); and to accuse the manager of being unfair or of concealed motives (offensive). All three behaviors represent defense or resistance. It is the demonstrated resistance that makes many managers uncomfortable. The more emotion that is displayed in the resistance, the more uncomfortable they become.

Negative emotional reactions are undesired short-term outcomes of confrontation that managers want to avoid. But managers also want to avoid the long-term effects that they fear these negative emotions may generate: damaged relationships with their employees.

Avoidance simply adds difficulty to the process of successful confrontation. It results in delay, and delay usually ensures that performance problems will become more complex and less manageable. Furthermore, by not confronting poor performance in a timely way, the manager can permit a performance problem involving a single employee to become an organizational problem that involves many others.

It is apparent that if managers could learn to confront in such a way that negative emotional reactions were minimized, they would be more likely to use confrontation as a coaching strategy. Coaching Process 2, improving performance, does limit such reactions.

Performance Standards

Another difficulty in setting the groundwork for successful confrontation is when performance standards have not been clarified with employees. Performance, to be directly managed, must always be performance against some standard. Of course, there are a few instances in which hard, objective standards probably are inappropriate and in which directly managing performance output makes little sense (e.g., in research laboratories and in creative arts such as painting or poetry). But most managers can and should establish performance standards. Without such standards, confrontation can become both senseless and arbitrary.

Many managers would be very surprised to learn how much ambiguity or lack of clarity exists among their employees in regard to their jobs. Telling people to be "more professional," "more proactive," "more friendly," and so on, does not tell them how to change, what to do, or how their performance will be measured. If they interpret vague guidelines differently from the manager and are reprimanded later, they may well feel misled or even sabotaged.

Aside from this, along the way, they will not be doing what their manager wanted or needed them to do.

Feedback

A third difficulty is caused by inadequate feedback. Feedback is the process by which managers should "close the loop" between expectations and performance. It is a process of both requesting information and giving information. By requesting information, managers obtain employees' perceptions of what and how well they are doing. By giving information, managers convey to employees their perceptions of the employees' performance.

The key characteristics of effective feedback are that it is *timely* and *sufficient*. When managers and employees say such things as "I wish I had known"; "Why didn't you tell me?"; "That comes as a big surprise to me"; and "When did we start falling behind?," feedback has not been timely. When they say "But I thought you told me earlier. . ."; "What you are telling me today sure is different from what you said yesterday"; or "When did we change the scenario?," the feedback has not been sufficient.

Feedback gives employees the opportunity to do what they want to do: take an active role in managing their own performance and ensuring that their performance meets the expectations of their managers. Feedback gives employees a basis for adjusting their performance. When feedback is timely and sufficient, confrontation may never be required. When feedback is not timely or insufficient, the coaching function of confrontation becomes more difficult.

Uncontaminated Appreciation

A final way to make confrontation unnecessarily difficult is to fail to show sufficient appreciation to employees for their work. If an employee feels unappreciated when beginning a coaching session on his or her performance, the employee is already primed to respond negatively and uncooperatively to the discussion. It is much easier for employees to be receptive when they are confronted about their performance if they already believe that what they do is known and appreciated by their managers. The key is to express appreciation for a task well done at the time that it occurs and without including any "buts" or negative information. Praise is difficult to hear when one is waiting for the other shoe to drop.

Successful coaching, of course, does not exist in a vacuum; it exists within the context of all the manager's practices. Coaching will be more successful to the degree that management practices are of high quality. This is particularly true of confronting. Managers have a much greater chance to achieve positive results from confronting if they avoid criticism, practice timely confrontation, establish clear performance standards, provide feedback that is timely and sufficient, and express uncontaminated appreciation to their employees. Given this basis, confrontation becomes a matter of creating and using Coaching Process 2, improving performance.

Coaching Process 2: Improving Performance

Process Similarities

In comparing Process 1, solving problems (Figure 3), with Process 2, improving performance (Figure 5), one notes that they are similar in many ways. Both have three interdependent stages. Stage II in both processes is focused primarily on developing information. Both processes employ basically the same skills, especially the information-developing skills such as attending, acknowledging, probing, reflecting, and summarizing.

Process Differences

It is primarily in Stage I that the two processes differ. In Process 1, either the manager or the employee may initiate the conversation, whereas in Process 2 the conversation is always initiated by the manager. It is the manager who perceives the need for a change in performance. Also, because Stage I in Process 2 begins with a confrontational statement, this process usually generates stronger resistance from the employee than does Process 1.

Another difference is primarily a matter of emphasis. All successful coaching conversations must conclude with the employee's

Process Stage I: Confronting/Presenting

Goals	Skills
Limit resistance and negative emotions	*Being Specific:* Giving clear statement of perceived performance problem.
Delimit performance topic	*Scoping the Problem:* Limiting statement to single problem.
Establish change focus	*Being Future Oriented:* Stating desire for change, not requesting reasons for failure.

Process Stage II: Using Reaction To Develop Information

Goals	Skills
Defuse resistance	*Dropping the Agenda:* Focusing on the employee's concerns, not on one's own.
Develop information	*Developing Information:* Attending, acknowledging, probing, reflecting, summarizing.
Agree on problem and causes	*Confirming:* Closing the loop; reaching mutual agreement on problem and causes.

Process Stage III: Resolving

Goals	Skills
Ownership of problem Next steps	*Planning:* Building strategies and agreeing on followup.

Figure 5. Coaching Process 2: Improving Performance

Positive relationship

Commitment

Reviewing: Going over key points of session to reinforce common understanding and ownership.

Affirming: Commenting on employee's strengths and positive prospects.

Figure 5. Process Stage III: Resolving (continued)

assuming the appropriate level of "ownership" of the problem. Ownership refers to the employee's acceptance of responsibility for carrying out the necessary actions or strategies to correct the problem. Stage III of Process 2 identifies ownership as a specific goal, because confrontation begins with a problem that was perceived by the *manager.* At the start of the confrontation, the problem is the manager's, *not the employee's.* One goal of confrontation is to transfer appropriate responsibility from the manager to the employee—or at least to develop a sense of shared responsibility.

Process Stage I: Presenting or Confronting

Stage I Goals

Stage I includes only the manager's initial statement of the performance problem and his or her expectations for improvement. The goals of Stage I are to:

- Limit resistance and negative emotions;
- Delimit the performance (coaching) topic; and
- Establish a focus on change.

Limiting Resistance and Negative Emotions

Managers do not confront employees about their performance to make the employees angry, upset, or depressed. In fact, managers often do not confront as often as they should because the demonstration of these emotions makes them uncomfortable. One goal of confrontation is to minimize the emotional reaction of the employee.

Delimiting the Performance Topic

A second goal of Stage I is to delimit (establish the boundaries of) the performance problem that the manager wants to discuss. This goal is related to limiting negative reactions. The more indefinite the confrontation is—or the greater the number of separate issues it includes—the more intense will be the employee's reactions.

One cannot, of course, predict what the final content of a coaching conversation will be. The manager may start out perceiving the problem to be X and, after developing further information, discover that the problem actually is Z. Still, whatever the final problem turns out to be, it is most efficient for the manager to start with the clearest possible delineation of one specific problem.

A manager may have difficulty in delimiting a performance issue if (a) the problem has gone on so long that it has multiplied or affected other areas or (b) if the manager is unclear about how to describe the problem because performance standards have not been established for the employee's job. We have already discussed many of the problems of avoidance and lack of performance standards. Another consequence is that they can lead managers to try to address a number of performance problems during the same coaching session. This not only causes confusion and negative responses on the part of the participant, it generally is futile in terms of solving the problems in the time available for the coaching session. The subject of the confrontation must be streamlined to fit the time available so that clear resolution can be reached.

Establishing a Change Focus

All successful coaching conversations are oriented toward change and the future. This orientation becomes an explicit focus in Stage I of Coaching Process 2. The success of coaching conversations depends on managers communicating to their employees at the outset that they want to correct specific problems, not to attack the employees or go over past mistakes.

Establishing a change focus helps to limit negative reactions. It is much less threatening for an employee to talk about what can be changed (i.e., the future) than it is for an employee to talk about what cannot be changed (the past). Of course the manager may be interested in the reasons why a problem has arisen. One goal of Stage II is to make these reasons more explicit. But the immediate goal of Stage I is to establish exactly what the manager perceives as the problem and how it can be made right, not why something has gone wrong.

Stage I Skills

Three skills are important in achieving the confronting/presenting goals of Stage I. These skills are: (a) being specific, (b) scoping the problem, and (c) being future oriented.

Being Specific

This skill is stating precisely what the standards are (e.g., "This is what is expected") and how the employee's performance differs from the standard ("This is what I perceive your performance to be"). A rule of thumb is that if the manager cannot describe exactly what he or she wants, there is no point in confronting the employee about it.

The following are some examples of specific statements of performance problems.

- "I expect everyone in the group to be present for our training sessions. I have not seen you at the last two sessions."
- "Unless there is an emergency, our rule is that travel requests must be submitted at least forty-eight hours prior to actual travel. I have three memos here from the travel office saying that you have not been following the rule."

Scoping the Problem

The initial confrontation or presentation should be limited to a single problem. Even if there are several examples of poor performance, the confrontation should start with the most recent example. Managers should not "save up" problems or examples and hit the employee with them in rapid fire (e.g., "I have had several complaints about your telephone manners, and I sometimes find that the telephones in the office are left unattended, and even when you are here I can't always talk to you because you are carrying on some private telephone conversation").

A manager who is uncomfortable about starting with a major issue may start with a less threatening issue, hoping to turn the conversation around to the important issue. This confuses the employee, takes up valuable time, and defuses the major issue. If there is more than one issue, the manager should identify the most important problem and solve it before proceeding on to a second problem—if there is time to deal with the second problem. If there is not, it should be left for another session. The description of the problem given above could be corrected as follows: "My boss complained to me this morning about the way you responded to her on the telephone. She said that she wanted to find me and you just said that you had no idea where I was and hung up." Note that this describes the most recent example of the performance problem and limits it to one specific behavior.

Confusion, resistance, and negative emotions tend to be limited (and the overall efficiency of the coaching session increased) if the manager and employee quickly agree on a concrete starting point. Scoping the problem in the confrontation presentation helps to establish this point.

Being Future Oriented

The skill required here is to include a phrase about change in the initial presentation or confrontation. Compare the examples that follow.

- "I need all members of the project present on time at our weekly status review. Why have you missed two out of the last three meetings?" (past oriented).

- "I need all members of the project present on time at our weekly status review. I'd like to know what you can do to make sure that you get to these meetings on time" (future oriented).

- "You missed our last budget-submission cutoff date by two days. What seems to be the problem?" (past oriented).
- "You missed our last budget-submission cutoff date by two days. What can you do to make sure you hit the date in the future?" (future oriented).

Being specific, scoping the problem, and being future oriented often decrease the amount of time needed to discuss a problem. Once presented with a clear definition of the problem and the manager's explicitly stated desire to fix it, an employee often will acknowledge the legitimacy of the manager's presentation and indicate what he or she intends to do about it. In terms of Process 2, the conversation goes directly from Stage I to Stage III, as the following example illustrates.

Manager: The error rate on your machine was above limits yesterday. What are you doing to bring it within limits?

Employee: I found a calibration problem in the input chute. I was accepting slugs that were outside the limits, but I've fixed it and I'm back to normal.

Manager: Good, thanks. Let me know if you run into the problem again. We may have to sit on the supplier a bit.

Putting the Skills Together

Stage I covers only the initial presentation or confrontation in Process 2. The following are complete examples of Stage I statements that employ all three skills.

- "I must know as soon as possible when you expect any delays in meeting the incremental deadlines for your project. In the last status meeting, you really surprised me with the news that the last shipment from the supplier was below standard and that you would have to slip the schedule for at least two weeks. How can you ensure that I get that kind of news immediately in the future?"

- "One standard that I hope all of us understand and work toward is that our customer gets the best service we can give—without exception. That standard includes our being inconvenienced if necessary. Yesterday BankPlus called me and said that you had been contacted about their loan-interface system going down, and you told them we couldn't do anything for them until after the weekend. They have got to have that system up the first thing on Monday. What can we do about it?"

- "Tidewater Shipping says that you didn't complete the asbestos-removal job. They say that you failed to strip the asbestos from the pipes in the generator room. Let's talk first about fixing Tidewater's problem and then about what we can do to keep this sort of thing from happening in the future."

Process Stage II:
Using Reaction To Develop Information

The most difficult part of Process 2 occurs in Stage II. This stage requires more discipline than any other element in coaching.

When employees are confronted, they will react. Their most typical reactions are to make excuses or to rationalize their performance; to take the offensive; to deny the existence of the problems; or to become passive or docile. Managers typically (unless they have been trained to do otherwise) will take issue with these reactions and exacerbate the problems rather than solve them.

For example, if the employee makes excuses or gives reasons for the problem, the manager typically will:

- Dismiss or refute the employee's excuses or reasons for the problem;
- Respond to the employee's excuses or reasons by restating the confrontation; or
- Reinforce the confrontation by quoting policy or presenting some other kind of argument.

If the employee takes the offensive and begins to attack, the manager often will:

- React to the employee's aggressive behavior by becoming more aggressive, too; or
- Retreat—back off from the confrontation.

If the employee denies the existence of the problem, the manager might:

- Become argumentative and attack the employee for not admitting the problem;
- Refuse to accept the fact that the employee has not acknowledged the problem and continue fruitlessly to solve a problem that has not been accepted; or
- Give up trying to solve the problem and communicate that the manager is also "giving up" on the employee.

If the employee becomes passive or docile, the manager will:

- Neglect to explore fully the employee's true perceptions of the problem or fail to gain the employee's full commitment to fix it; or
- Criticize the employee for not having recognized and fixed the problem before the manager had to bring it to the employee's attention.

It takes enormous discipline for a manager to use whatever the employee does or says to develop information about the problem and to help the employee to explore his or her perceptions of the problem. The guiding rule in confrontation is: *Do not fight the employee's reactions; fix the performance problem.*

Stage II Goals

The goals of Stage II are to defuse resistance, develop information, and agree on problems and causes.

Defusing Resistance

Each time managers confront employees, they introduce the possibility of change. Each time they introduce change, they introduce the possibility of resistance. Improving performance requires that managers accept the responsibility for managing the resistance they have created. One major step in managing resistance is to dissipate the negative emotions associated with resistance. By encouraging the employees to explore their opinions, feelings, reasons, and excuses, managers can help them to transform their negative feelings into verbal behavior.

Developing Information

Another goal of Stage II is to develop all the information necessary for the manager and employee to be able to reach a mutual understanding of the problem and its causes. A manager starts a confrontation session with a point of view; the manager has an opinion about a performance problem. There is always the possibility that the manager's perception is not accurate. By encouraging and stimulating the employee to explore issues and causes—from the employee's point of view—the manager may discover more about the true problem.

Agreeing on Problem and Causes

The final goal of Stage II depends on the successful achievement of the first two goals. Reaching this goal may require several iterations through Stages I and II.

For clarity in illustration, the coaching processes are described in this book as linear processes. In actual practice, they are cyclical and iterative. In the case of confrontation, it often is this cyclical and iterative quality that contributes to the success of the process. For example:

- *Stage I:* The employee is confronted with the manager's perception of the performance problem.

- *Stage II:* The employee reacts to confrontation—usually by giving reasons for the problem. The manager drops his or her own agenda and uses the employee's reaction to confrontation to develop information and a mutual understanding of the problem. Two things can occur at this point: (a) no new information is developed, and the performance problem remains as the manager initially perceived it; or (b) new information is developed, and the manager modifies his or her perception of the performance problem.

- *Return to Stage I:* If no new information is developed, the manager returns to Stage I and repeats the initial confrontation. If new information is developed, the manager returns to Stage I but modifies the confrontation to fit his or her new perception of the problem.

- *Return to Stage II and Further Iterations.* Stage II is then repeated. Stages I and II will be repeated so long as the statement of the problem continues to be modified and until the manager believes that the most important problem has been identified accurately.

Stage II Skills

The skills for Stage II are dropping the agenda; developing information; and confirming.

Dropping the Agenda

The first and most difficult skill in Stage II is the ability to mentally lay aside one's own agenda for the time being and to focus specifically on the employee's reaction, whatever it may be. This requires that the manager attend fully to the employee with one purpose in mind: to use the employee's reaction as the temporary agenda of the conversation.

A manager may be uncomfortable with the idea of dropping the agenda, even temporarily. It may seem as though talking about what the employee wants to talk about is "getting off the subject" or "a waste of time." But it is only by responding directly to what the

Reviewing

In the process of concluding a confrontation session, the manager must ensure that all the important aspects of the conversation are mutually understood. This means that time should be allotted for carefully going over a statement of the topics covered during the conversation. Reviewing should include such things as a summary of the topics covered, misunderstandings that have been resolved, and a final test to ascertain that the problem and its primary causes have been identified accurately. The following are some examples of reviewing.

- "I started this conversation by asking you about the technical review that our client has been requesting. My understanding was that we had agreed that you were giving it priority treatment. We seemed to have misunderstood each other about that, so you have been giving time to your other projects while still working on the review. Also, you indicated that you were running into problems with the data-analysis branch and not getting a timely response from that group. But I think you understand now just how important it is to finish that review. What we need to do now is figure out what can be done to complete it as quickly as possible."

- "I guess we got off on a pretty rocky start with this conversation. I had my point of view and you had yours. It seems to me now that we have agreed on the basic issue: the contract really doesn't permit you to tell the contractor exactly what to do. I felt that you were not giving the contractor much guidance, and you believed that you were abiding by the contract. So what we have to change is the contract. In the meantime, though, we need to come up with a temporary solution."

Reviewing prepares the conversation for its next development: planning how the problem will be resolved.

Planning

Planning has two parts: strategies to resolve the performance problem and a follow-up process to keep the manager informed about progress. Some managers do a very credible job of confronting only to lose the payoff by not giving sufficient attention to planning. Planning is the way in which the coaching conversation is translated into action steps. Planning does *not* mean that the employee merely states that he or she will correct a problem. Intentions to correct a problem and stated resolves to try harder are of limited functional value.

The manager should always develop with the employee some specific action steps for responding to the problem and a schedule for following up these actions so that the manager is kept informed of the progress. The employee should take primary responsibility for developing action plans. The following are some examples of planning statements.

- "Give me your ideas on what we can do to get you more involved with the contractor. I have a number of suggestions, but I'd like to get your ideas first."
- "O.K., our plan is for you to review with me the critical meetings on the new information system that are planned for the week. We will agree on the ones that you must attend and the ones that you will attend if you can work them into your schedule. We also will take a few minutes each Friday to see how this procedure works for you."

Affirming

Employees may leave performance-related coaching sessions with some negative feelings about themselves and their managers. It is particularly important that the manager end a confrontation session with some positive comments about the employee's performance. These comments can relate to the total nature of the employee's performance as well as the contributions that the employee made during the coaching conversation. The goal is to end the conversation with the employee committed to improvement and confident in his or her ability to improve. Examples of affirming statements are as follows:

- "I know that this conversation has been tough for you, but I think we're on track again. I have no doubt that you'll turn the project around."

- "You certainly have given me a new slant on the problems on the floor. I know now that you haven't been happy with the way we've been using our quality inspectors either. With the plan you've suggested, I think we'll be in a lot better shape by next week."

- "Your technical work has always been excellent. I think you now know how important it is for you not to have negative relationships with other engineers, and I believe that the plan we've put together is going to work because you want it to."

The next sections of this chapter will provide two examples of confronting. As with the examples for Process 1, each example will be accompanied by comments that identify the stages of the process and the skills used.

Examples of Coaching Process 2: Improving Performance

How To Use the Examples

The examples in this section are intended to help you to transfer your learning about the confrontation-coaching function to on-the-job application. The examples illustrate the goals, stages, and skills of confronting. The suggestions that follow will help you to make the best use of these examples.

1. Before you read through an example, review Coaching Process 2 and the special skills associated with each stage (Figure 5).

2. Cover up the right column of the examples and test your own ability to identify the stages and skills.

3. Practice making the confrontational statement (Stage I) in your own words and test your statement to see that it meets the criteria of being specific, being scoped, and being future oriented.

4. After you have gone through an example once, read through it again and substitute your own responses for the ones the manager gives in the example.

Example 1: Confronting Unsuccessful Performance

Successful confrontation of performance problems can result in clarification of performance expectations, identification of performance deficits, strategies to improve performance, and commitment to continuous improvement.

Confrontational Conversation	Comments
M: Thanks for coming in, Terry. I know that I'm interrupting your schedule but I've discovered a problem that we need to solve. The engineering department has indicated that your people are not processing the finished problem reports that engineering is giving you at the 90 percent weekly rate that you and I established with them last month. I would like to accomplish two things with you this morning. One, how can we catch up and get rid of the backlog? Two, how can we make sure that we meet our commitment to engineering in the future?	**Stage I: Confronting** *Being Specific* *Scoping the Problem* *Future Oriented*
S: I'm doing the best I can with what I've got. I know I'm behind. I know engineering is ticked off. But, frankly, I feel like I'm between a	Employee reacts by defending himself and begins to give reasons for problem.

rock and a hard place. I had no idea that I would have to face the kind of complications that have come along since our agreement.

M: So, some things have come up that were not in the picture when we set the 90 percent goal.

Reflecting
Stage II: Using Reaction To Develop Information

S: "Some things" is an understatement. The specs for cover sheets were changed and made retroactive for all problem reports not returned to engineering. This meant that all the packages in process had to be reviewed, the old cover sheets removed, and the new ones added. Each new cover sheet also requires a summary statement, so we had to do those. We tried to write them ourselves in order to take some of the load off engineering, but they wouldn't initial most of them because they didn't like the way we worded them. They didn't like the suggestion of human error because of the repercussions for their department. In some instances they couldn't give a specific reason why something broke, and it goes against their training to put down anything they can't prove.

M: So you've run into a slowdown because the cover sheets had to be changed.

Reflecting

S: That's right. But that isn't all.
More than 40 percent of the
problem reports that engineering says
it has closed out have to be returned
to engineering because of errors. So
we have to wait for engineering to
make the changes and return the
papers to us before we can complete
our job.

M: So you think that engineering is   *Reflecting*
taking too much time to return the
papers to you.

S: It's not that they take too much
time. It's that there are too many
reports that have errors when we get
them.

M: Let me see if I've got it all.   *Summarizing*
One, you know that we aren't
meeting our goal of 90 percent
weekly closeout on problem reports.
Two, one reason for the slow up is
that the cover sheet was changed,
and this required your people to go
back over work they had already
completed. Three, the new cover
sheet requires a summary statement,
which you had to add, and engineering has had some problems helping
you with that. Fourth, there are
errors in over 40 percent of the
problem reports sent to you from
engineering, so those have to be
returned for corrections before you
can process them.

S: That's about it. I had hoped to bring the problem under control before you had to get involved, but I didn't make it.

M: I know the feeling. I don't like to tell my boss about problems if there is any way I can fix them first. If we have identified all the causes, what can we do now? What have you tried so far?

Self-Disclosure

Open Probe
Open Probe

S: I've met with the systems engineers and explained the new cover sheet. They understand that the report is going to bounce untii they give a summary of probable cause. We agreed that no one ex-pects them to say "human error" unless they have very strong support for it. We've also agreed that when they don't have a clue about the failure, they can use "operational failure." I know this sounds hokey, but the system will not accept a blank. We can't close out a paper without a probable cause.

M: It sounds fine to me. Do you ex-pect this tactic to speed things up?

Acknowledging
Closed Probe

S: It already has.

M: What else have you done?

Open Probe

S: We've started to separate the problem reports by system and

process them in bunches. This way
we stay with electrical for a day
and then do mechanical, and so on.
When we go from one system to
another, it takes more time to get
into it.

M: Good. Is there anything else?   *Closed Probe*

S: At the moment, that's it. But there
is one other reason why we've fallen
behind schedule. We have the most
inexperienced quality people reviewing the papers. We have to keep the
old hands on the floor where the
work is being done.

M: So that's another reason for the   *Reflecting*
slipped schedule: that you are
using inexperienced people to do
the job.

S: Right. They are all good people
and they are all working really hard.
But they are not familiar with about
80 percent of the stuff they have to
review.

M: Given what you have already
done, when can you take care of the
backlog? When do you expect to   *Closed Probe*
start meeting the goal?   *Closed Probe*

S: Right now, the goal is unrealistic.
With my current resources, we will
get 75 percent, and that's with the
changes I have made.

M: What else can you do?

Open Probe

S: I need more qualified people, but I mean qualified! Just giving me more people won't help. I don't have time to train now. I think I'm getting as much from engineering as I can expect. But if they hadn't changed the cover sheet, I think I would have come close to the goal.

M: So here is where you are. You've educated engineering about the summaries of probable cause on the cover sheets. You've changed the way you process the paper and are doing it by system in batches. But even with the changes you have made, you can process only 75 percent of the weekly input of problem reports. That means we are accumulating a 25 percent backlog per week. We can't live with that. We have to meet the 90 percent rate.

Summarizing

**Phase I: Confronting
Second Iteration of
Phase I**
Being Specific

S: That's a tough one, but I don't know where else to go from here.

M: O.K., what if we put an engineer in your area to take care of all the papers that lack only a statement of probable cause on the cover sheet? That would free your people up to get on with the rest of the review process.

Stage III: Resolving
Resourcing/Planning

S: That would be worth trying,
provided you can get the engineer. I
know what kind of response I would
get at this point.

M: I will get you the engineer.   *Resourcing/Planning*
Give me a list of the qualifications
you need—or even the person you
want—by two o'clock.

S: You'll have it. I know of at least
three engineers who would do just
fine.

M: The next thing is to upgrade   *Resourcing/Planning*
your people quickly. I'd like you to
talk to Ed in the software group. He
had to upgrade his new people a
few years ago. From all reports, he
put together a pretty slick system.
Give me your best ideas by the day
after tomorrow for putting your
people on a fast training track.

S: O.K.

M: One last thing that I want you   *Resourcing/Planning*
to do is to look at the steps that you
now take to process a problem
report. You may find some slack.
Evelyn in the productivity office has
a technique called "work simplifica-
tion" that has gotten a lot of positive
results. Study it and give me your
results in a week. Now, we've
covered a number of plans. I think   *Confirming*

that it would help if you played them back so we know that both of us are on the same track.

S: You're going to get me an engineer who will work in our office to take care of the papers that just need probable-cause summaries. Next, you want me to meet with Ed and put together a fast training plan for my new people. You want that the day after tomorrow. Finally, you want me to contact Evelyn and run a work-simplification check on our process for handling problem reports. You want those results in a week.

M: I'd say we are in agreement on your next steps. I think we've made a good start at solving this problem. We'll get you an engineer, you'll develop a fast training plan and try the work-simplification strategy. I know that your job is tough right now, but I believe that you can handle it. I understand the problem better, too. If it is humanly possible, we'll reach that 90 percent goal.

Acknowledging
Reviewing

Affirming

Example 2: Confronting an Employee To Accept a More Complex Job

---

Confrontational Conversation	Comments
M: Chris, you've been working in estimates for a year now. I've observed your performance and I've had positive reports from your supervisor about your performance. We are opening a branch in the eastern part of the state, and I'd like you to take over estimates there. It will be a one-person show for the time being.	**Stage I: Confronting** *Scoping the Problem*
S: That's very flattering, but I don't know if I'm ready for it. You know, I was in the field until last year. I've had to learn estimating from the ground up. Every day I learn something new. Without a supervisor around, I think I could get into hot water in a hurry.	**Stage II: Using Reaction To Develop Information**
M: So you see yourself as still on a learning curve.	*Reflecting*
S: I've learned a lot, and with a little more time—say another six months—I think I'll be ready. But right now, I just don't know. I wouldn't want to make a mistake that costs the company a lot of money and lose my job.	
M: So your main concern is underestimating a job and being	*Reflecting*

blamed for losing the company
money.

S: Well, it can go both ways.
You can also lose the company
business by being too high in your
estimate.

M: I see; you still think that   *Summarizing*
you've got a lot to learn. You believe
that you need someone around to
talk things over with before you
make a decision. You're afraid that
you may cost the company money
by either over- or underestimating a
job. And I guess you feel that you
are in danger of losing your job if
you make a mistake. Is that right?

S: Yeah, that's it. And when you say
it that way, it sounds like I'm some
kind of coward.

M: It's not easy to do an estimate   *Self-Disclosure*
on your own. The first one I did over
20K, I didn't sleep a night through
until the job was done and we had
our money. Let me test a few things
with you. Would you want the job if   *Closed Probe*
you thought you could handle it?

S: Sure, I'm planning to move
up someday. I just don't think I'm
ready yet.

M: O.K., you want the job.   *Acknowledging*
Tell me what would help to make   *Open Probe*

you feel comfortable about
doing it.

S: I'd like to start out with jobs that
cost no more than 10K, and I'd like
to have someone review my work for
the first half-dozen jobs I do.

M: My goal is to get you on your   *Resourcing*
own as soon as possible. At the
rate we are growing, I will need
you to start training some new
estimators in a couple of months.
Here's my proposal. You take the job
and take responsibility for all jobs
that are 10K or less. But it's your
call. If you want to take on something bigger, do it. I'll give you three
months. After that I expect you to be
on your own. Any job that the
southern branch gets, you estimate it.
You will work on all estimates, but
I'll sign off on anything over 10K that
you send in. Also, we expect you to
ask for help any time you need it—
from me or anyone in the office.

S: Well, I'd be crazy not to try.
When do you want me to start?

M: I want you at the branch on   **Stage III: Resolving**
the first of the month. There is   *Planning*
one thing that you might do in
the meantime. Pull out all of last
year's power plant jobs that we
estimated. That's the kind of thing

that will be your big jobs. Pick out a couple and analyze them. Then come to me with any questions you have and we'll go over them.

S: O.K., I'll do that and get back to you by the end of next week.

M: We've covered a good bit here. I don't want any surprises, and neither do you. Tell me what we've agreed on.

Confirming and Reviewing

S: I'll report to the new branch on the first of next month. I'll be expected to be on my own within three months. Until then, I will be responsible for jobs of 10K or less—unless I choose to go above that. I do all the work on job estimates, but you will review and take responsibility for the ones over 10K. I can get whatever help I need from you and anyone else in the office. And you want me to review the power plant estimates and bring in two of them with questions.

M: That covers it. I know that you'll do an excellent job for us. If I left you where you are now, I think you would soon be frustrated with the limited responsibility. You know as much about what we do in the field as anyone around here, and that's 90 percent of estimating.

Acknowledging Affirming

Key Learning Points for Chapter Four

Coaching Processes 1 and 2 have these important similarities:

- Both have three interdependent stages;
- Process 2 employs many of the skills from Process 1, especially the information-developing skills such as attending, acknowledging, probing, reflecting, and summarizing; and
- Stage II in both processes is focused primarily on developing information.

Processes 1 and 2 differ in the following ways:

- In Process 1, either the manager or the employee may initiate the conversation. In Process 2, the conversation always is initiated by the manager, who perceives the need for some change in performance.
- Because Stage I in Process 2 begins with a confrontational statement, this process most often stimulates stronger resistance from the employee than does Process 1.
- Ownership is emphasized more in Process 2 than in Process 1. Confrontation begins with a problem perceived by the manager. At the start of a confrontation, the problem is the manager's—*not the employee's.* One goal of confrontation is to transfer appropriate responsibility from the manager to the employee—or at least to develop a sense of shared responsibility.

Summary of Coaching Process 2: Improving Performance

The key points to remember about the process and skills in Coaching Process 2 are:

1. Coaching Process 2, improving performance, has the following stages and goals:

Stage I: Confronting or Presenting:

- Limit resistance and negative emotions;

- Delimit the performance topic; and
- Establish a change focus.

Stage II: Using Reaction To Develop Information:
- Defuse resistance;
- Develop information; and
- Agree on the problem and causes.

Stage III: Resolving:
- Ownership of the problem;
- Next steps;
- Positive relationship; and
- Commitment.

2. Coaching Process 2 describes what typically goes on in successful coaching conversations that have the function of confronting deficit performance problems or of confronting opportunities for moving employees from successful to higher levels of performance.

3. The general flow of the process is the same, whether the problem is unsuccessful performance or a move to a higher level of performance.

4. Stage II, using reaction to develop information, is the most difficult stage in all coaching conversations. It requires the special discipline of dropping one's own agenda and using special skills to develop further information.

5. All stages of the process are interdependent, and there typically are iterations from Stage II back to Stage I and back to Stage II, etc., until agreement is reached on the problem and how to solve it. Overall, however, the process is directional and moves toward specific results and closure.

6. It is not the specific content of Process 2 but the process itself that leads to the general results of successful coaching.

7. Confrontation is a positive process and should not be confused with criticism.

8. Confrontation often is made more difficult than it needs to be because managers: (a) do not establish clear performance standards; (b) do not give sufficient and timely feedback on performance; and (c) do not express genuine appreciation to employees for their contributions.

Chapter Five:
Coaching and Superior Leadership

I n this book, "coaching" means conversations that managers have with employees in carrying out the functions of counseling, mentoring, tutoring, and confronting. But coaching also can mean other managerial actions and conversations with employees. In this sense, coaching is used to denote a person's whole *style* of managing. It most often is used to describe managers who display three general characteristics in their practices: (a) They recognize the limits of trying to *control* employees and try, instead, to build commitment; (b) they have extensive personal contact with their subordinates; and (c) they have a strong developmental bias toward their subordinates.

It is apparent that much of this is included in the functions of counseling, mentoring, tutoring, and confronting. To carry out these functions successfully requires that managers build commitment through extensive personal contacts that have a strong developmental bias. In other words, to carry out the four functions of coaching successfully, managers must have a coaching "style." Not all managers are coaches, but all *superior* managers are.

What Superior Managers and Leaders Do

During the past eight years, I have conducted a series of studies to determine what superior managers and leaders do. The distinction between a manager and a leader is that "manager" is an assigned organizational role, whereas "leader" is a role that can be assumed by anyone. Thus, not all managers are leaders and not all leaders are managers.

However, people in organizations tend to identify managers as leaders more often than they do any other set of employees. By studying superior leaders in organizations, we inevitably study managers. I believe that my conclusions about superior leadership can, therefore, be applied to managers.

Superior Managers

There are eight sets of practices that distinguish superior managers. They are as follows:

1. *Action Focus:* The manager is focused on making things happen, on meeting objectives, and on solving problems that hinder progress.

2. *Performance Focus:* The manager is focused on the highest possible standards of quality and productivity.

3. *Improvement Focus:* This is a measure of the degree to which a manager is focused on maintaining continual improvement and on ensuring that there are concrete improvement goals in the group.

4. *Contact Focus:* A manager with this focus stays in touch with all members of the group and with the users of the group's products and services.

5. *Relationship Focus:* This describes the manager who develops and maintains positive work relationships within and outside the group.

6. *Development Focus:* This manager is focused on developing the competencies and careers of the group members.

7. *Team Focus:* This describes the manager's concern with building cooperation and commitment to common goals within the group.

8. *Character Focus:* This describes the manager's practice of displaying at all times the highest personal ethics and work standards.

What is striking about these sets of superior management practices is just how many of them suggest the three elements of a coaching style (commitment, contact, and development); the four coaching functions of counseling, mentoring, tutoring, and confronting; and various coaching actions such as encouraging, giving feedback, applauding success, demonstrating a skill, challenging, etc.

The superior management focuses of contact, relationship, development, and team all relate directly to coaching. This relationship is even more obvious when one looks at examples of specific practices included in some of these sets.

Under the relationship focus, for example, we find these specific practices:

- Typically confronts problems in work relationships in a positive and timely way;
- Encourages others to be frank and open in their opinions;
- Typically treats the opinions of others with respect;
- Usually is honest with others about his or her own ideas and opinions; and
- Typically maintains easy and informal relationships with subordinates.

Every one of these practices is essential for conducting any of the coaching conversations of counseling, mentoring, tutoring, and confronting.

The practices included under the development focus are even more explicitly coaching practices. They include:

- Regularly coaches subordinates to develop present and future competencies;
- Always helps subordinates to cope positively with disappointment;
- Usually delegates extensively and avoids micro-management;
- Regularly educates subordinates about senior management's values and ways of doing business; and
- Ensures that all members of the work group are regularly involved in training activities to enhance their present and future performance.

Thus, there is much similarity between coaching and superior management practices. When we set out to describe what superior managers do, we end up describing them as coaches.

Superior Leaders

My studies of superior leaders suggest that these leaders share six sets of common practices. These six sets are:

1. *Establishing a Vision:* Superior leaders create expectations for significant and lasting achievement. They give meaning to work by associating even menial tasks with valued goals.

2. *Stimulating People To Gain New Competencies:* Superior leaders stimulate people to stretch their minds and their wills. They freely share their own expertise and keep people in touch with new resources.

3. *Helping People To Overcome Obstacles:* Superior leaders help others to overcome obstacles. They help others to find the courage and strength to persevere in the face of even the greatest difficulties.

4. *Helping People To Overcome Failure:* Superior leaders help people to cope with failure and disappointment. They are quick to offer people who fail new opportunities.

5. *Leading by Example.* Superior leaders are models of integrity and hard work. They set the highest expectations for themselves and others.

6. *Including Others in Their Success.* Superior leaders are quick to share the limelight with others. People associated with superior leaders feel as successful as the leaders.

The correspondence between superior leadership practices and coaching is compelling. Each of the six sets of superior leadership practices could be described as recommended coaching practices.

For example, these are the specific practices included under "establishing a vision."

- Generally succeeds in helping people to believe in the lasting importance of their work;
- Regularly helps others to accept new challenges;

- Generally helps to keep others from feeling bogged down in unrewarding tasks;
- Consistently encourages people to work toward challenging goals; and
- Typically inspires others to make personal sacrifices in order to get the job done.

This book previously has described the indicators of commitment as focus and self-sacrifice and has indicated that one of the four strategies for building commitment is for managers to communicate clarity about their vision, goals, and values. The set of superior leadership practices listed above works toward building a focus and self-sacrifice through clarity.

Superior leadership practices included under "stimulating people to gain new competencies" are:

- Often encourages others to try creative ideas;
- Often suggests to others new ways to approach problems;
- Regularly puts others in touch with sources of new information and ideas;
- Freely shares his or her own expertise with others; and
- Often leads others to develop new insights.

These clearly correspond to the coaching functions of mentoring and tutoring.

A final example of the parallels between superior leadership and coaching can be found under the set of superior leadership practices "helping people to overcome obstacles." This set includes the following practices:

- Typically challenges others not to quit—no matter what the obstacles;
- Often helps others to find new resources of personal strength;
- Often helps others to find creative ways around obstacles;
- Typically gives special support to others when they face difficult obstacles in their jobs; and
- Regularly calls attention to the strengths of others.

The answer to the question "What do superior managers and leaders *do*?" is "They coach."

Conclusion

Coaching is not an option for managers. It is a large part of their basic managerial functions. It is clear that superior managers and superior leaders engage in coaching—and they do it well. The good news is that managers can learn the set of management practices that we call coaching. Most of these practices are included in the functions of counseling, mentoring, tutoring, and confronting. These functions, in turn, are carried out by means of series of coaching conversations.

All coaching conversations are in the form of one of two basic processes: Coaching Process 1, solving problems, or Coaching Process 2, improving performance. Learning and using these processes can be powerful strategies for anyone who wants to become a superior manager.

A Note to Trainers

University Associates is currently developing a trainer's package to accompany *Coaching for Commitment*. This will consist of a Trainer's Manual, a Participant workbook, interactive videotapes, and ancillary materials. Watch for these materials in the UA Resource Guide later this year.